Help

Help

Simon Amstell

◪ SQUARE PEG

1 3 5 7 9 10 8 6 4 2

Square Peg, an imprint of Vintage,
20 Vauxhall Bridge Road,
London SW1V 2SA

Square Peg is part of the Penguin Random House group of companies
whose addresses can be found at global.penguinrandomhouse.com.

Penguin
Random House
UK

First published by Square Peg in 2017

Penguin.co.uk/vintage

A CIP catalogue record for this book is available from
the British Library

ISBN 9781910931547

Text design by Secondary Modern

Typeset in 11.5/16.5 pt Plantin by Jouve (UK), Milton Keynes
Printed and bound by Clays Ltd, St Ives plc

Penguin Random House is committed to a sustainable future
for our business, our readers and our planet. This book is made
from Forest Stewardship Council® certified paper.

For my mum, who birthed me out of her body
and then helped me with my jokes.

NOTE

The text that follows is new writing interspersed with excerpts from previous stand-up tours:

no self, london, 2007

do nothing, dublin, 2010

numb, london, 2012

to be free, new york city, 2015

Some names have been changed to protect privacy.

CONTENTS

CONTENTS

We're all damaged in a way. We're all sort of damaged. Are you damaged? You look kind of damaged . . .

do nothing

I was tricked into this book. I was asked if I'd be interested in having the transcripts of my stand-up published, and rather than saying, 'Thank you, but I don't think there's any need to do this,' I said, 'These words must be written down.'

And who for? For people who don't like hearing stand-up out loud? I was told part of the deal was I'd have to record an audiobook and then there would be a promotional tour, where I'd read my stand-up from a book.

The only way I could think to get out of this situation was to write something new and so horrifically personal that no one could think of it as anything other than an heroic act of self-annihilation.

It's scary telling the truth in a book. In stand-up you can say anything as long as it's funny but in a book you can say anything. I've written some things that aren't funny at all and I feel exposed. But better to expose your absurd 'self' than try to protect it. It feels good to have all these stories out of my head and in a book where they can't confuse me any more. I got them out of me.

shy, funny, lonely

I was so shy as a child, I would cling to my mother's leg and scream if she tried to leave me somewhere like a birthday party or a school. I was terrified of anything that wasn't being at home. I remember Adam Edwards inviting me to his fifth birthday party and I said I was busy. 'Sorry, Adam, let me check my diary. Oh, it's just impossible, I'm in Berlin.'

I really hoped I'd have a sister at some point because I was going to be too shy to find someone to marry. 'If there could just be someone born in this house who I could settle down with, that would be ideal.'

My mum and dad were advised by Mrs Posner, at the school parents' evening, to send me to a Saturday-morning stage school called 'Stardust', to bring me out of my shell. I guess I must have said, 'I don't want to go to Stardust,' as I remember my mum saying, 'What if I promise to sit outside, the whole time you're there?' I have no memory of anything that happened in that class, just walking in and looking back at my mum sat in the corridor.

Yet something magical must have happened. I guess a bunch of Stardust was sprinkled over my terrified head because after a few months, I began to feel comfortable volunteering to be on stage. I learned that performing in front of a group of people was safe, though I still wasn't able to deal with one person at a time. At this point, I may have unconsciously decided that finding one person to be in a relationship with was going to be impossible so getting better at performing in order to become famous was essential.

And then I'd never be lonely because there would always be fan mail.

I'm quite lonely, let's start with that.

I bought a new flat about two years ago. In this flat, in the bathroom, there are two sinks. I thought that would bring me some joy. It is a constant reminder.

And so what I have had to do, this is what I am doing now in my life, I am actually doing this – I'm using both sinks. Now, every day I brush my teeth in the left sink and in the right one, I mainly cry.

do nothing

At eleven I was too old for Stardust and began attending the Harlequin Theatre School and Agency. I may not have continued my Saturday-morning stage-school education but my favourite TV show, *The Big Breakfast*, had just started and looked like the most fun anyone could have. More than fun, it was unconventional; it looked like freedom. I still didn't have any conscious understanding of why I needed to be so free but I took every class that Harlequin offered.

Presenting a TV show wasn't taught at Harlequin so I studied Chris Evans. I began to dress like him, even though he dressed like a clown. I hosted my own version of *The Big Breakfast* in my bedroom, doing 'links' into a camcorder, while holding a clipboard and making jokes about members of a crew who cheered me in my head.

I did anything that I thought could be a way in to the television. Despite not being able to sing, I got the role of Pharaoh in *Joseph*, in the annual school musical and I put all my energy in to being as funny as possible, while repressing some very confusing feelings for Joseph.

I learned to juggle and became very upset when my mum refused to let me have a unicycle for my birthday. Eddie Izzard had been a street performer before he became a famous comedian and if I couldn't unicycle I felt it could hold me back.

I went to see TV shows being filmed. My mum and I went to watch *The National Lottery*, even though it only lasted fifteen minutes. I was thrilled by cameras moving across a floor. We went to watch *The Vanessa Feltz Show* together and I felt sure that despite it being a show presented by a woman in her forties for women in their forties and called *The Vanessa Feltz Show*, I should really be the host.

The subject up for debate that day was: 'Should I Murder my Husband?' At the beginning of the show, the floor manager told us that the best opinion that day would win a bottle of champagne. So there was everything to play for – should she or shouldn't she murder her husband? Twenty minutes go by and people say some very interesting things and then I stand up and say, 'I think you *shouldn't* murder your husband, cos you could go to prison.' And I won a bottle of champagne.

do nothing

At thirteen, I did my first stand-up gig at the Harlequin biannual variety show. Two years earlier, I had sung and danced in the *Chicago* number – 'Razzle Dazzle' – wearing a silver sequinned waistcoat and matching top hat. I was the stand-in for a former student who didn't have time for the rehearsals but was apparently going to perform the song on the night. I assumed he wouldn't turn up but when the night came, he was placed centre stage and I was given a spot on the side, which was sold as generous. There was no need for me to be included but I could dance along in the corner, dressed as a small version of the main singer, like a little monkey person.

By the time my second chance at making a name for myself at the Harlequin variety show came around, I wouldn't even let puberty get in my way. My body kept trying to tell me that I fancied boys and I had other stuff to deal with – my bar-mitzvah, my parents' divorce, the biannual variety show – I didn't feel there was also time to fall for Leonardo DiCaprio from Baz Luhrmann's *Romeo + Juliet*. Better to begin a stand-up career and get into the television. Having now checked the dates, it seems *Romeo + Juliet* didn't actually come out until I was seventeen so this is a false memory and I apologise.

I think the truth is, I managed to repress any sexual thoughts from even awakening until I was seventeen and rendered helpless by the moving image of Leonardo DiCaprio's hair falling over his eyes as some fish swam by.

It's possible I could have seen *What's Eating Gilbert Grape* at thirteen but I think I only discovered Leo's early work much later. I would go to the video shop and rent out every film with DiCaprio in. I remember thinking, There's going to be a record of this, it's a worry – people will say, 'You're in love with Leonardo DiCaprio, it says so on your video club card.'

When *Titanic* came out, I went to see it four times. Aside from the sexual attraction, I connected to the story of money getting in the way of love. My mum had remarried and I didn't like this new stepfather character. I took my mum and grandma to the cinema to show them that true love was more important than financial security.

At the end of the film, my grandma said, 'How could she leave such a rich man? He gave her a huge diamond and she left him for a boy who lived under a bridge? All he had was a pencil!'

Along with my DiCaprio premonition, I definitely had some complicated feelings for one of the boys at Harlequin. I hoped I was just impressed with his piano playing and ended up being groped in a shopping centre by his girlfriend. I wasn't sure why it was happening. She just kept grabbing my penis. We were supposed to be shopping. I was happy that she liked me because I thought it meant I was as attractive as her boyfriend, even though I couldn't play the piano. And if she liked me, was it possible that he could want me too? But did I actually want him or did I just want to learn the piano? I definitely didn't want to be molested by this girl in a shopping centre but that's what I got.

Meanwhile, two years after the 'Razzle Dazzle' debacle, the drama teacher told the whole group that there was a problem with the biannual variety show. He said 'the big tap number has been scheduled next to the big ballet number and both dances will be performed by the same dancers, in different shoes'. Rather than changing the running order, or making the bold choice of presenting a ballet number featuring children in tap shoes (or a tap number that nobody would hear), they thought if they could just cover the shoe change with something in front of the curtain for five minutes, everything would be fine.

I'd been watching a lot of stand-up comedy

on late-night Channel 4. Mainly quite peculiar American and Canadian comedians, at what must have been the Montreal Comedy Festival. They offered the same sense of freedom I felt watching *The Big Breakfast*. I don't think I understood what was going on, or why any of it was funny, but it felt like something exciting was happening in Canada.

All I really knew was that stand-up comedy was one person on stage, having an incredible time, doing whatever they wanted and receiving a wild amount of what sounded like love.

I had a powerful impulse to get that five-minute spot. These Saturday-morning drama classes were where I felt the most safe and happy. I think I knew that if I could be a comedian, I could really be in control of something.

I said to the drama teacher, 'What about stand-up comedy?' and he said, 'Do you mean *you* doing stand-up comedy?' I said 'yeah', casually, like it was a fairly reasonable suggestion and incredibly, he *didn't* say, 'Are you sure, Simon? You know stand-up comedy is quite tricky and you are a child.'

I have a wall in my flat now of various
comedic inspirations (Woody Allen,

Richard Pryor, Lenny Bruce) and the whole wall is a lie. I didn't know who any of those people were when I was thirteen. If there was any truth to that wall, it would just be a sign that reads: 'Parents divorced, learned to juggle to stop mother crying.'

to be free

Why didn't somebody put a piano in front of me as a child? Then I could have learned the piano, I could be in a bar, playing beautiful songs, requests . . . There are no requests with juggling, other than, 'Don't juggle!'

numb

So at thirteen, a vulnerable age, when a lot of young people go into themselves and become shy, I'd done shy already and stand-up comedy didn't feel that scary. What felt scary was being fascinated with the way Leonardo DiCaprio's hair fell over his eyes, even though I hadn't seen it yet. I must have known it was coming. 'Quick! We need something to distract from all that beautiful hair blowing in the wind of the future.'

In preparation for my first stand-up set I wrote some jokes and also stole bits from the Channel 4 shows I'd been watching. One guy had a bunch of enormous cards with words written on them. He showed a card with the word 'THIS' to the audience, and said, 'Would you look at "THIS"! Has anyone ever seen "THIS" before?' Then he grabbed another card with the word 'THAT' on it and shouted, 'What about "THAT"? I bet you weren't expecting "THAT"!' I thought, This is brilliant. And did his act word for word.

I also wrote some original material. I have a strong memory of one specific line: 'You're born, you go to school, you get a job, you get married, you have children and then you die. What's the point of that?'

Not a funny line but I thought it would be a good one to begin this book with, to show that I was an incredibly profound, existential child prodigy. I found the VHS tape of the show and the line isn't there. I think I may have made the memory up.

According to the tape, which we must

trust, I walk on stage, very confidently despite a multicoloured waistcoat and say this:

> What about these environmentalists, ladies and gentleman? These green people, who care more about recycling their toilet paper than actually using it?
>
> *the harlequin variety*
> *show – queen's theatre,*
> *hornchurch, 1993*

It makes my stomach tense watching it. Why is this boy making fun of people trying to save the planet? Why is he doing some bits in an American accent? There must also have been some old seventies-style comedians still on TV because some of the jokes I did were about Irish and German people. Did I even contemplate the meaninglessness of life at thirteen or was I just a normal child? No, I was doing stand-up at thirteen; I must have been profoundly deep and certainly troubled. Maybe there was a rehearsal where the drama teacher suggested my line wouldn't go down that well, because everyone in the audience had jobs, children and would die. I think that must be it. I was a censored child genius who understood the absurd, meaningless nature of existence – and not just an oddly dressed xenophobe.

There was just enough laughter to make me feel like I really wanted to do it again. Watching the tape now, it seems that a lot of that laughter was nervous and confused. It occurs to me that I hadn't actually been introduced as a comedian, so they probably thought I was doing a monologue from a play about a racist.

After that, I did stand-up at a local charity show, I entered competitions for new comedians and I was booked for my first TV gig on *Good Morning with Anne and Nick*, doing an impression of Dame Edna Everage. I was in the television. I'd never be lonely again.

acceptance

acceptance

This happened when I was fifteen. But I think it's too odd a story if I was fifteen so better if we say I was eleven.

I was in my grandparents' house and I used to have quite a good relationship with my grandma, she used to really validate me in my life. I would do little drawings and doodles and she'd say, 'Oh that's nice.' I'd do another drawing: 'that's nice'; another drawing: 'oh, that's nice'. And at one point I distrusted the consistency of her reviews.

So I did a deliberately bad drawing to see what she would say. She said, 'Oh that's nice.' And I thought, I can't deal with this inauthentic sycophant!

So one day . . . And I know *now* that I did this because I wanted to do something where she couldn't validate it, where she couldn't say 'oh, that's nice', but when I did it, it was purely unconscious. One day I ran up to my grandma and I mooned my grandma. But I was only eleven. I'm just eleven.

It wasn't even like a cheeky, playful little moon and
run away . . . it was a violent bend over, here's my
arsehole, Grandma, and apparently a bit of balls
as well, a little bit of balls.

do nothing

Not only did I not know why I was mooning my
grandma in the moment of the mooning, I also
wasn't sure while talking about it on stage. I now
think of this as a story about a young gay person
in Essex testing whether something shocking
and unacceptable could still be met with love.

I think everything I've ever done in front
of an audience has been a version of showing my
grandma my bottom. Frustrated and, I suppose,
scared by the conventional, I've spent a lot of
energy, on stage and off, fretting about how much
of who I am will be tolerated before I'm rejected.

When I was eighteen I was working as a
presenter on the kids' cable channel Nickelodeon,
introducing shows like *Rugrats* and feeling worried
that I may be a homosexual. There were no gay
people that I knew of at Nickelodeon but I wasn't
really looking. I was mostly just very happy to be
a presenter, reading from a clipboard, talking to a

puppet and saying 'Here's *Rugrats*' with enough enthusiasm to make the crew cheer.

But what to do about being gay? I secretly got on the train to Paris, to see if boys were worth the hassle of ruining my life. I told no one. I was living on my own in a flat in Ilford, having been thrown out of the house by my stepfather because my mum didn't like *Titanic*. I bought a *Time Out* guide to Paris and hid it in the back of my wardrobe, just in case anyone came round.

I thought the fear of being gay could be responsible for creating these overpowering gay feelings. This made sense at the time, even though people who are scared of heights don't also have an intense sexual urge to sit on a roof. I thought if I just went somewhere and did something, I could move on with my life. And the boys I fancied tended to look like girls anyway so I thought, If I can just find a girl with short hair and no breasts, I'll probably be all right. It was a great plan and it would have all worked out, if it hadn't been for those pesky dicks.

I packed a small black T-shirt, hair gel and contact lenses. Because I thought, That's what they'll like – a skinny boy with spiky hair and the illusion of good eyesight.

As soon as I arrived, I changed in the

bathroom of the train station. Looking at myself in the mirror, as I put in my contact lenses, it freaked me out that nobody knew I was there. I thought, I could just die here and nobody would know why – 'All he had on him was hair gel ... What was his plan?' I remember talking to myself in the mirror.

'Are you OK?'

'I think so, are you OK?'

'I don't know, maybe we're OK.'

I got in a cab to the club I'd circled in my *Time Out* guide – 'Le Queen'. There was a woman on the door who said, 'It opens at ten and doesn't really get going until one.' It was eight o'clock.

I nervously walked up and down the street, mumbling to myself for hours. I was hopefully going to kiss a boy but I was also going to be very tired.

Eventually it was an appropriate time to arrive at the club. I went in and wasn't sure what to do other than drink a lot. I'd never been to a nightclub before. I went on a lads' holiday to Magaluf at seventeen with some equally awkward friends but we were too scared to go clubbing. We didn't understand how anyone could just walk in to a building and then transition from standing still and talking to stopping the talking and beginning the dancing. We discussed this for many hours while sitting on a wall outside a club.

I assumed that because I was young and skinny, someone in Paris would approach me and tell me who I was but no one did. This is so strange to me now because that vulnerable eighteen-year-old boy, even to this day, is my type. I wish I'd been there for me.

I did a lot of walking around the enormous club over the next two hours and eventually saw a really cute boy. I felt just brave or drunk enough to go up to him and say the French for 'will you kiss me?', a phrase I'd written on a small piece of paper and memorised. I tapped him on the shoulder and he quickly turned around. I asked, *'Allez-vous m'embrasser?'* And he kissed me.

I still remember thinking, as he was kissing me, Oh yes, gay.

It felt like the kind of kiss that I was supposed to be involved in. And then it stopped. He started speaking in French and tried to give me his phone number before running off. I should have learned the French for 'I'm only here for one night' or followed him until we found a translator.

I still can't believe my French wasn't better when just two years earlier I achieved an

'A star' in my French GCSE oral exam, for sentences like, *'mon père travail dans le banque'*. My dad didn't work in a bank but I couldn't figure out how to say 'my father runs a courier company' and I thought, Who's going to check?

The boy left, with no idea of what he'd done for me. I thought I could probably go home at this point but then decided that I'd come all this way and my hair was still quite pointy. I felt confident now, I knew exactly what I wanted, and half an hour later I saw somebody else – not quite as cute, but he could speak English, which was useful. I asked, 'Can we go somewhere?' He said he had some people in his apartment but had an idea. I asked, 'What's your idea?' And then he took me to a canal, where I lost my virginity.

And then – and this is the most disgusting and romantic sentence I have for you – we washed the cum off our hands in the fountains of Paris.

Thank you.

But here's the sad bit. I think if I'd slept with the first boy I kissed that night, I could have got on the train home and come out immediately. Instead, because the chemistry wasn't quite there by the canal, I was left thinking I could probably live without that kind of thing and didn't touch another person for three years.

I started going to a terrible nightclub in Romford with my old school friends, who had since learned how to transition from standing still and talking to stopping the talking and beginning the dancing. I felt it was very important to stay in contact with my old school friends in Essex, perhaps so I could avoid being myself in London.

Even when I spoke about this years later on stage, I didn't deal with the reason why I went clubbing in Romford, just the frustration.

. . . Three years between the ages of eighteen and twenty-one, three years! Every Saturday night in Romford for three years because nobody told me that London was close!

And you had to wear black trousers to get in; black shoes, an untucked shirt . . . And I don't like it when the dress code is 'basic dick'. I think it's restricting.

One time, I don't know if I was being rebellious or if I just thought it would be OK, I wore black trainers. I thought that would be all right and the bouncer looked at me and said, 'You can't come in dressed like that, you look like you've come from a gym.'

'Which gym do I look like I've come from?'

He was such a basic human being, to him there were only two forms of dress: 'club' and 'gym'.

do nothing

I wish I could go back and give myself a hug.

Two years later, I was about to be sacked from Nickelodeon for becoming too sarcastic for kids' TV. The boss told me he'd have to ask me to leave unless I could go back to perky. I remember being very depressed doing some Christmas links because a year had gone by and I still hadn't worked out how to make them funny. The director sent me home because I looked so sad. She was quite compassionate but the puppet was very angry. I was terrified that it was the end of everything I'd ever wanted. I was so young and looked even younger; I didn't know where else I could be employed.

Then, just before I was officially asked to leave, I did an interview with the pop star Mandy Moore (the last in a long line of 'new

Britney Spearses'). I think a combination of not having a full crew available for the shoot and laughing with a researcher beforehand while reading Mandy Moore's official biography meant that I felt just relaxed enough to discover a new way of being on camera that felt completely natural. I felt funny. I think I knew I was doing an impression of Ruby Wax but somehow also felt like I'd found my self. I edited the interview and sent the tape to various agents. Joanna Kaye was incredibly enthusiastic, which was quite fortunate because none of the other agents got back to me and I was about to be fired. Halfway through our meeting, Gaby Roslin from *The Big Breakfast* walked in and I felt like everything was going to be OK.

Joanna took me on but the man in charge of Nickelodeon told me I would definitely have to go. He said I could stay until I found a new job, which was very upsetting at the time but now seems incredibly kind. Meanwhile, Joanna put me up for a new pop show on Channel 4. She felt sure that I was exactly what they were looking for but also suggested I get some new clothes as they were 'looking for someone stylish'.

At twenty-one, I was presenting *Popworld* on actual, terrestrial television. I was so happy but realised quickly that at some point, on the television, my co-presenter was going to say something like 'Justin Timberlake is very attractive', and I would have to say something like, 'I don't know what you mean'.

So two months into *Popworld*, I decided to go to Miami to properly figure out who I was. I think I'd seen the film *The Birdcage* and thought, That's where they are. I didn't know anything. I could've gone to New York, San Francisco . . . I could have gone to London.

I went to a club on the first night I arrived but didn't see anyone I fancied, so I went back to the hotel. On the second night, I went to another club and saw somebody with the kind of transcendent hair that made my teenage years so confusing.

I got very drunk and circled the room. He was standing next to someone and I felt I shouldn't interrupt. I kept going round and round, getting more and more drunk until I eventually was able to go up to him and I say, 'Are you with him?' He said 'no' and we ended up in the back seat of his friend's car, being driven back to his apartment. It didn't need to be any more exciting than this but then he took out his penis and cheekily smiled at me. At first I thought, I can't do this, I'm on Channel 4.

But then I felt scared I might not get the opportunity again and as I was sucking his penis, I remember thinking, Oh yes, gay.

His apartment was really cool and he was slim but incredibly toned, which made me notice for the first time that I was just slim.

He was twenty-eight, his name was Kurt and he had the accent of all my childhood crushes. I don't know what we did that first night but it must have been good because I stayed for three nights. I was so pleased to finally be having sex in a bed.

We spent the entire time alternating between sex and old episodes of *The Golden Girls*. I was very fortunate to have arrived in America during a *Golden Girls* marathon.

At some point I thought, I've booked a hotel, I can't waste the room. And so we said our goodbyes. Half a day later, I began to miss him. I called and he said he'd been missing me too. I went back to the apartment and we spent the rest of the week together.

Despite all this, I still couldn't quite say that I was gay. I told Kurt I thought I was probably bisexual and he asked, 'When you masturbate, what do you think of?'

I said, 'Right, it's a good point.'

For some reason, we ended up talking about celebrities being in the closet and how if there were confused and terrified children in the world committing suicide, it was not OK for someone in a position of influence to be silent.

At the end of the week, Kurt drove me the airport and we hugged goodbye. Something real had happened.

A few days after I arrived home, my mum and younger brother Robert come over to my flat. I was determined to tell them about this boy but after about two hours of talking about Miami and just responding 'no' to the question, 'did you meet any nice girls?', my mum went to get something from the car. Standing by the window, I said to my brother, 'I met a boy in Miami, what do you think? I'm about to tell Mum, shall I tell her?'

He said, 'No.'

When she came back, I said, 'I didn't meet a girl in Miami but I did meet a boy.'

She said, 'You're joking.' And I said, 'No.'

'Tell me you're joking.'

'No.'

'Are you joking?'

'No.'

'Tell me you're joking.'

'No.'

'Tell me you're joking!'

'I'm joking.'

'Are you?'

'No.'

... My mum finally said, 'Let me just think about it for a few days', like she was going to figure something out.

I said, 'Didn't you know? I went to a drama club, I did tap dancing.'

And she said, 'Don't stereotype!'

I was told not to tell anyone else, especially anyone in the family, and I cried that night. I had to make myself cry because I wasn't used to it but it felt like the right thing to do. I sat cross-legged on my bed and wished my mum could have been better. I think really she must have known because when I was sixteen she asked if I'd been searching for gay porn on my stepdad's computer. Luckily I'd just seen an old film called *A Guide for the Married Man* where Joey Bishop gets away with sleeping with another woman by repeatedly denying that the woman lying in their bed is even there. So when my mum asked about the porn I just kept repeating phrases like 'of course not', 'what are you talking about?' and 'I don't know why it's on his computer, maybe it's his!'

My mum and I have a good relationship but there's a detachment, an inauthenticity to every conversation. I feel like I should be able to tell her anything but there's this sort of awkwardness . . . and I've realised it's because I came out of her vagina and that's sort of always there, you know?

'Oh have you done your council tax, Simon?'

'Mum, I came out of your vagina; let's not pretend that's a normal thing to have happened. I came out of your vagina, I sucked on your tits; you want to talk about tax?'

And with my grandma as well. It's awkward because my mum came out of her, I came out of my mum, It's a Russian doll of awkwardness.

do nothing

I decided I needed to tell my agent who I was, to check if I was going to be able to stay in show business. I walked into her office and asked if we could have a quick chat. I was nervous but came up with the sentence – 'How do you feel about bisexuality as a career move?' She said, 'This is great, gay people are always the most talented', completely ignoring the fact that I was bisexual.

I said, 'What about . . . ? I don't want it to be the main thing about me, you know? But I'm on this pop show and if Miquita [the girl I was presenting the show with] says she fancies someone, I want to be able to say that too.'

Joanna's response: 'Well, you should just do that then.'

On my first day back at work (before we started recording), in an attempt to make an announcement that didn't seem like a big announcement, I managed to come out to everyone in such a garbled way that no one heard.

I looked around the room and noticed the only person who had actually spotted what had happened was a new runner. He was looking at me, wondering what I was going to do next. He seemed to suggest with his eyes that I try again. So I did and this time everyone heard but no one believed me. Miquita, who grew up in London around all kinds of exciting people, looked at me and said, 'Trust me, you're not.'

On air, I attempted to subtly drop in the occasional sentence about liking a boy, which was incredibly clunky, as I was trying to make something that at the time was quite a big deal not a big deal. Eventually it became as irrelevant as everything on that show but it took a while.

Meanwhile, after months of emailing and talking on the phone with Kurt, we arranged to meet up again in New York. We decided that if this went well, he'd come to London and move in with me, which I agreed to, mainly out of politeness.

I didn't know how to say 'that seems a bit crazy, don't come to London', so instead I said, 'Yeah, you should come to London because I live in London!' The other problem was I lived in Ilford, which was not London.

Before he arrived, I went into a mild panic that my flat wasn't what he'd be expecting and started pulling up carpet and sanding the floors. He was leaving this beautiful, wood-floored apartment in Miami for a flat in Ilford with net curtains – net curtains that weren't there when I moved in, I put them up.

He waited a month before saying, 'You know this isn't London.'

I said, 'It's on the Central Line.'

Living with Kurt meant there was now an enormous lie I was telling everyone in my family. Either I must have been too subtle on TV for anyone to notice or none of them were watching.

I had always talked to my aunt and grandma on the phone, at least once a week, and I began to feel sad about the bit in the conversation where I *wouldn't* say that I was living with someone. And because I wasn't very good at talking without being funny, when my aunt would say, 'What did you get up to last night?', I'd say, 'I went to a big gay nightclub!' And she'd laugh. This went on for a month, until it was clear that I wasn't joking and she summoned me to her house.

I searched the internet for things to say to family members to reassure them that everything would be fine and had some key sentences in my pocket. I knew it would all be quite strange and new for everyone but I'd never felt so free and hoped they'd see how happy I was. When I arrived, my tense-looking aunt opened the door and said, 'Don't make a fuss!' I'm not sure what she was expecting me to do. I was taken into the living room, where my mum was waiting with my uncle. The doors were closed so their children couldn't hear what was going on and then my aunt started crying and didn't stop for two hours.

It was so overwhelming, I forgot my sentences from the internet. My aunt's tears made her the most vulnerable person in the room and suddenly the only thing of any importance was finding a way to stop the crying. I think the hope was that I would change my mind. They were very worried I'd be bullied, that I'd have a terrible life and I was sat there thinking, This is the worst thing that's happened so far.

My uncle, an accountant, gave me a book written by a client of his called *A Gay Man's Guide to Safer Sex – Fingering, Fucking and Fisting*.

'Thank you, Uncle Graham.'

He must have flicked through it because he then asked, 'Are you douching?'

I was twenty-one and didn't know what douching was, so I said, 'Of course I'm douching, we're *all* douching!'

Eventually I was allowed to leave as long as I agreed I wouldn't tell my grandparents because it would kill them.

Because it's genuinely believed in this family that when my mum got divorced, which was quite a drama, it was the direct reason for my Grandpa becoming diabetic.

do nothing

How can there still be homophobia, when Elton John wrote *The Lion King*? What does he have to do?

to be free

I hated having to lie to my grandparents. I missed a Christmas with my family because I couldn't bring my boyfriend. Eventually, I said to my grandma on the phone, 'I keep not saying something to you.' And when I finally managed to say it out loud, she panicked and hung up. And died.

(She didn't die.)

My grandparents actually turned out to be much less traumatised than anyone. My grandpa was particularly sweet with a photography student I went out with. They discussed exposure rates at a family lunch and I almost cried.

Then there was my dad, who I didn't get the chance to tell because my mum wanted to see the look on his face.

I have a father who found religion when my parents divorced. I guess he was searching for something structured and meaningful in his life. For a while he was just canoeing.

I wouldn't have the problems I have with my father if he'd just been a bit better at canoeing. Or drowned.

to be free

After she told him, I was asked to come over and he suggested some kind of therapy. He denies it was electroshock therapy, but he definitely gave me a flyer for something.

At one point, a couple of Orthodox Jews knocked on the door, and walked in. I thought, I'm about to be taken away by Jews and electrocuted. But they were collecting for charity, so I was OK.

I said (to my father), 'What is the sentence about homosexuality in the Torah that's the problem?' He didn't really want to discuss it so I said, 'Well, I looked it up and one of the problems seems to be that it says you need to put me to death.'

He said, 'Well, that's not my responsibility.'

So not, 'Let's disregard that sentence, it was written a long time ago by fallible human beings . . .' 'Yes, that is what should happen, Simon, but I've got a lot on.'

I studied parts of the Torah so I could find something to make me feel comfortable with who I am. I found, in the book of Samuel: 'And Jonathan made a covenant with David because he loved him as himself. Jonathan took off the robe he was wearing and gave it to David. They kissed each other, and wept together, until David became great.' Unfortunately at that point the Bible pans to a shot of a fireplace but . . .

to be free

I can't feel too annoyed with these people. They just happen to be from a particular generation, living in a particular place, and from their perspective, a hardcore sex book and electro-shock therapy were generous gifts.

I think I knew that none of it was personal. My aunt, uncle and father also treated my brother like a deviant loon for finding a non-Jewish girlfriend. This was handy for me, as I found it much less painful to be angry with them for upsetting him than for rejecting me.

At my grandpa's seventieth birthday party, I caused a major drama and then spoke about it in my stand-up, which also didn't help.

Everyone was there apart from my brother's girlfriend who he's been with for about four years. She was not there on account of a couple of the family members having a problem with her not being a Jew. We mustn't judge them for this. This is just because they personally have a very strong belief in racism so . . .

I say, in as sweet and polite a way as possible, 'Isn't it a shame that my brother couldn't bring his girlfriend tonight? It's sort of a shame, isn't it?'

And they get quite defensive and say, 'Well, why *isn't* she here? We thought she *would* be here; why isn't she here?'

And I say, 'I don't know. Isn't it because of that time you said "she *can't* be here"?' I ask, 'Just explain to me, why is the belief more important than the feelings of a human being?' And it's so sad because she's a brunette, she could pass.

Their perspective was that it was a terrible misunderstanding and the one time they did meet her, she hadn't said hello to them. And I had to explain that she's the shy, new guest coming into this family, we are hosting her, we have to say 'hello' first, that's how it works. Can't we learn from Lumière the candlestick holder in *Beauty and the Beast* who sang 'be our guest, be our guest' not 'is she a Jew?'!

I really tried hard with my family. My aunt said, 'It's not our fault, it's your mother! *She* would rather that he was with a Jewish girl.'

And my mum said, 'No, that's not what I've said, I've said that in an *ideal world* he would be but I'm happy that he's happy.' Which sounds more positive but she was creating a whole other world there where he was with someone else. So I said, 'We have to let go of this idea of an ideal world, the world is how you perceive it, it's ideal if you want it to be ideal, and they are in love, surely love is the ideal.' And I won a bottle of champagne.

do nothing

The problem with needing people to love you, despite who you are, is that you end up subtly compromising for them and so internalise their prejudice and *their* rage. Rather than let them reject you, you allow all their nonsense to live inside you. You don't realise it but you agree to feel uncomfortable about this bit of yourself too, just slightly, just enough to keep them in your life. You settle for being mildly content with who you are, rather than proud or thrilled, and any attempts at love will be thwarted by this refusal to love yourself completely.

I should have known that impressing my family with my romantic life was going to be unlikely but when I broke up with Kurt after two years, I felt a real need to be a 'good gay'. I didn't want to be predatory, or promiscuous or any of the judgemental words I used to shame myself away from any kind of fun.

Sex can just be fun, it can just be fun, it can just be fun. No one ever says, 'Oh, you're playing all that tennis, where's it leading?'

do nothing

At school I'd been such a good boy. My mum always told me that as a baby, I was 'no bother'. As an adult I was a bother and I wanted to minimise this as much as possible. I became so befuddled by what was appropriate or good that when I was twenty-four, I made the mistake of assuming I was in a relationship with someone who I'd had sex with twice.

He eventually felt the need to say to me, 'I'm worried you think this is a relationship.' I said, 'Yes! What else would it be?'

He told me he wasn't ready for a relationship and didn't want to hurt me. He tried to kiss me goodbye and I was so angry and confused I refused the kiss. I really liked him and couldn't understand how I'd been dumped by someone who'd approached *me* at a party, he came up to me. I thought, If you're not ready for a relationship, you should stay at home and prepare.

My friend suggested he maybe just wanted to have some fun, so I called him and left a message on his voicemail saying, 'Hey I think we should just have fun, let's have fun. I'm fun!' He didn't call back and I felt sad for a year.

I should have had a lot more sex in the past, when there were these opportunities that I missed because I was so frigid and terrified. I remember being at a party, and I was in a room with three attractive men, and one of them turned to me and said, 'We should have an orgy!' And I said, 'Ha! This is a nice room.'

And I can't go back, even if somebody suggested an orgy now . . . What I bring to a social setting is humour and nobody wants to be sarcastically fellated. People don't want to be ironically fingered, you've got to commit to that.

You'd think that if you had some regret about not having more adventure in the past, you'd make sure you had it in the present. I went to see this piece of immersive theatre, where you wander round five floors of a building and it's dark, people are wearing masks, there's this feeling of anonymity, like anything could happen. There's a bar area with an actor playing the role of a barman – although he was also a barman.

He came up to me and said, 'Would you like to go on an adventure?' And I said, 'What would that involve?'

He wouldn't tell me, so I walked away terrified until I realised, this is a fictional adventure. I go back after about half an hour and say, 'OK, I'm ready. Whatever it is, I'm ready for my adventure.' He speaks to the lady in charge. He comes back and says, 'It's too late.' And that's the end of that story.

What am I going to do? I'm going to lead a mundane life and then just die. I think I'm OK because I live in London but the truth is you can't really appreciate anything if you live in London because there's so much going on. Like this tonight, right now, this is a pretty intimate space . . . and I'm quite famous! But it's just another night for you; it's probably one of *three* interesting things

you're doing this weekend. People in
Sheffield would lose their minds!

to be free

I really wanted to be a person in a long-term relationship and eventually found someone who I couldn't leave. He was very young and beautiful. I was twenty-five and deranged.

I decided his glowing skin and shiny hair meant he was pure and I would need to do my best to pretend to be. He was a very sweet, loveable person and what follows are the worst parts of the relationship. What makes for good stand-up tends to be the bits of life that go wrong. So while reading the rest of this chapter, please try to imagine two people who were quite often having a lovely time.

We were in a supermarket together and a
friend of his who I hadn't met before
approached us and because I hadn't met this
guy before I got instantly nervous. The guy
then says, 'What are you up to?'

And I say, 'A bit of shopping; we've got a pineapple'.

An hour passes and then the boyfriend says to me, 'What's wrong with you? Why do you always have to try to be so funny?'

I said, 'It wasn't funny, it was factual.'

He said, 'You deliberately chose the most humorous object in the trolley.'

'Well, I'm gifted.'

do nothing

I completely lost myself. He taught me how to dress but eventually, didn't let me leave the flat unless I was wearing what he'd suggested, so I looked great, but in prison. I once met him on Oxford Street. I was wearing a colourful woolly hat and he looked incredibly troubled by it.

He said, 'What are you doing? You need to take that off.'

I said, 'It's OK, I don't think it's cool, it's funny, because I'm funny.'

He needed me to take the hat off, so I took it off. And then I was gone, which I thought may be a good thing because I'd become quite interested in Buddhism where losing the self is nirvana. If you can attain 'no self' then there can be no suffering – no hat, no self, no suffering. But I didn't become a transcendent Buddha, I became an abused housewife with a cold head.

```
The only thing I've really learned
about relationships is that you
have to make the person feel
special because we do have egos ...
And with everything that I was
reading about Buddhism, that
there's no self, you can't bring
that stuff into your relationship.
You can't say to the person you're
with, 'I love you but really if you
think about it, I could love
anyone.'
```

no self

Understandably, he felt I should be less detached and more in love. I wasn't at a point in my life where I could let myself be vulnerable enough to love or be loved. I wouldn't have even known

what that sentence meant. All I knew was that if
I couldn't love a boy this beautiful, I probably
couldn't love anyone.

I believe he had 'anxious
preoccupied attachment'. Which
means that he needed me to be a lot
more present than I could be,
listening to every word, which would
have been fine except I had
'dismissive avoidant attachment' –
which means that often I'd be in a
room with him and say 'what are
you doing today?' and just as he
started to answer, I'd walk out of
the room.

. . . really the blame lies with me. I
was not committed enough in the
relationship, and I tried my best to
pretend to be committed. I would do
little things all the time to show how
committed I was, little things, like
buying a flat with him.

no self

Just before we bought the flat, I tried to tell a friend how worried I was but didn't yet have the capacity to be sincere, so tried to make my anxiety funny – 'Should I really be moving in with him? What's the alternative? I can't be alone in my flat for ever, it's decorated, there's nothing left to do. I can't keep wandering around London, buying new cushions, there'll be too many cushions.'

I was terrified of ending up alone for ever, even though when I was five, I learned a powerful lesson which I must have forgotten. I was at the back of the garden and a chair collapsed on my finger. I screamed for help but no one could hear, so I stopped screaming because I realised, I'm alone.

We had quite different expectations regarding money. He'd been brought up with money and I didn't yet understand the concept of buying things that weren't necessary.

I was only twenty-six. Someone could have said, 'Have fun, have sex, meet some nice people you want to spend time with. Don't move in with someone whose intense beauty and passion bewilder you.'

'Why don't you ever buy me flowers?' he once asked as part of an argument about why I never did anything lovely. I didn't know why I hadn't ever bought him flowers but eventually came up with, 'I didn't grow up with flowers – we didn't even have a vase. If people brought flowers to the house, we'd have to plant them in the garden. "Thank you for the flowers, next time could you bring food?"'

He once spotted a photograph in a bar that he liked. I called the bar the next day to see if the photograph was for sale. It was a black-and-white A4 print that could be purchased for £250. I was shocked. The lady explained that it was a limited-edition print. I hadn't heard this phrase before and thought, for £250, I could take a lot of my own photos and choose what's in them. I told him the whole story, thinking he'd find it sweet and funny. He looked sad and said, 'Why didn't you just buy it?'

I understand now that he just needed some kind of gesture that meant I loved him.

Jealousy was also a problem. I had an old photo album in a cupboard, featuring photos of my first boyfriend and a couple of other boys I'd seen more casually before we met. He needed me to throw the old photos away. Why did I need them? He suddenly had no respect for limited-edition prints. I threw the photographs away. His need for them to be gone was greater than my need for them to be kept. He coped with his jealousy by unconsciously lowering my self-esteem. I don't think he bullied me, although I'd never really been bullied apart from at Nickelodeon by a puppet who was supposed to be a bit snarky with whoever he was presenting with, which would have been fine if when we finished shooting, he hadn't said to me, 'I meant that.' Eventually I realised I was giving the puppet his power by believing he existed and began to stop making eye contact with an insecure man's arm.

There wasn't much bullying at my school, but there was a child who arrived for the sixth form with a very large penis and he would chase people with it.

It was a terrifying time. I
imagine it was the largest in the
school because nobody ever
challenged it with their own penis.
Even the teachers said,
'There's nothing we can do.'

no self

One day we were looking for a restaurant and I suggested Cafe Emm. He looked suspicious and asked, 'How do you know about Cafe Emm?' I'd been on a couple of dates there, but I couldn't say that because my past was now in a bin.

A few weeks later at a New Year's Eve party someone came up to us, who I didn't recognise at first. He said, 'We had a date at Cafe Emm!'

I just stood there and smiled. It was so out of my control, it didn't feel real. I felt like I was stuck in a play where I'd just have to wait for my boyfriend to say his furious lines, so I could respond with my passive lines and then watch him storm off stage. Then the curtains would come down, surely, please, who's in charge of the curtains?

I followed him out of the party. He was screaming at me but it was New Year's Eve and there were fireworks going off so I couldn't hear anything he said. It felt incredibly cinematic, so I imagined the play had been turned into a film and waited a long time for the credits.

I went to my mum for some advice but her advice is only ever practical. All the furniture in this flat was his, so when I said, 'I just don't know who I am any more in this relationship, I've got to get out of it', she said, 'You can't split up with him; you'll have nowhere to sit.'

no self

I stayed with him for another two months, during which I met a psychotherapist at an event I was asked to host. When I wasn't on stage introducing people, I said, 'I know you can't tell me what to do but I'm in a relationship and I'm really stressed, what should I do?'

She said, 'You should leave him.'

I said, 'Oh.'

'Yeah, you don't need that in your life. What do you need that for?' She gave me what felt like official, medical permission to leave.

However, the question then became: *how* do I leave? I still felt it *should* work – we were just two human beings in a flat in Hampstead, if this couldn't work, what hope was there for the Middle East?

I was eventually told – by *another* psychotherapist – that this was silly and finally felt able to end it. My boyfriend and I woke up together. He asked if I was going to have breakfast with him. I said I was OK. I stayed in the bed until he was in the shower. I sat on the sofa in my pyjamas until he eventually walked into the living room. I said, 'I don't think we're making each other happy.' He said, 'I knew this was coming' and agreed. He was calm. I was free.

But then I went to New York and he was angry. How could I go to New York in the middle of this break-up? For me, it felt like a good time. He thought the relationship hadn't meant anything to me, that he was just some guy who had stuck around. As part of the break-up he said he needed some money to move out. I think he just wanted proof that the relationship had actually happened. If he couldn't make me love him, maybe he could make me hate him. But he couldn't crack me. No matter how insane and upsetting the situation became, I remained a detached, highly compassionate psychopath. I was in Edinburgh, doing a show that was partly about him. I was terrified a reviewer would quote one of the lines. I could have dropped the jokes but jokes are not easy to come by and the show was already too short.

We were both seeing therapists in order to make the break-up less traumatic. Unfortunately, therapists tend to side with the person they're treating and it became more traumatic. This was until my therapist told me about 'The Drama Triangle' and 'The Winning Circle'. I called my ex from my bedroom in Edinburgh, with a diagram in front of me, featuring a triangle and a circle, along with the key sentence – 'I'm OK, you're OK'. We spoke in a vulnerable, assertive and caring way (these were words from 'The Winning Circle') about how we'd both ended up being one or more of the following things on 'The

Drama Triangle' – Victim, Rescuer, Aggressor. What followed was the most intense meta conversation I've ever been involved in. When he was aggressive, I asked him if he could transition to 'assertive' and I was able to do this because I was allowing myself to be 'vulnerable' enough to say things like, 'when you talk to me like that, it scares me'.

Thanks to our time in 'The Winning Circle', we were finally able to speak to each other. I was now just angry with myself for letting it all happen. I was also too scared to be anything but vague in my next show about the lesson I was finally able to receive.

I got in this minicab and starting telling the driver about it. He said to me, 'Well, is there anything you can do about this bill?'

And I said, 'No, there's nothing I can do.'

He whispered, 'Acceptance.'

'What do you mean, whispering wise cab driver?'

And he explained so absurdly simply that if there's nothing you can do about something, you do nothing.

And in that moment, the feeling of injustice, the frustration was lifted. There was nothing to do.

do nothing

Even after the break-up, I would see him at the odd party and feel scared that he'd disapprove of who I was with or what I was doing with my life. I remember going into a panic while cutting up a melon in someone's kitchen. He walked in and I said, 'Hi! Do you want some melon? Look at this melon!' He didn't want any melon. I kept going, 'Have some melon! Delicious melon; why wouldn't you want the melon?'

He said, 'Because you're not really offering me melon, are you?' He could always spot when I was using fruit as a defence mechanism. Half an hour later, my cousin called me. I went outside because I knew it could be bad news. He told me my grandma was dying. I stood in the street, feeling something much deeper and less familiar than anxiety. I went back in to the house to get my coat. The atmosphere at the party felt suddenly insane. Someone tried to talk to me and possibly, for the first time that I can remember, I didn't start performing. I must have looked quite sad but she didn't seem to notice. I saw my ex-boyfriend on a sofa near the door and sat next to him. I said, 'Hi, I'm about to go. I want you to know that the relationship we had meant a lot to me. It wasn't nothing. So thank you.' And then I got up and left.

me but better

At twenty-seven, despite having become everything my thirteen-year-old self wanted to be, that relationship, along with an obsession with the self being an illusion, meant that I wasn't very impressed. If I was funny, it was the writing and editing; if I was attractive, it was the fame and lighting. I suppose the real problem is we're not significant, are we? I learned how to be myself by being on stage. But to be on stage, you have to believe that you're special. The Buddhist principle of 'no self' therefore causes problems. I was safe if I was special but I couldn't be special if I wasn't a self.

Who was I? Who? This is the kind of question you can spend a lot of time with if you live alone and don't have a job.

I thought a cat would ease my loneliness. But then I realised a cat is not going to make me feel any less lonely. A cat is only going to provide a mascot for my loneliness. So if

anyone does come round they go: 'Oh,
you've got a cat, are you lonely? Ah . . . what's
he called?'

'Solitude.'

do nothing

What I realised, having been in this relationship,
was how much of my time had been spent with
him and now I didn't have quite enough friends.

I think I have three but one I'm
not that keen on. You know I look
through my phone and I have 150
names in it but these are not the
people who I would normally
phone and say 'hey, let's have
lunch today', these are the people
whose names are only in my phone
so that when they call, I don't
answer.

no self

You just have to make plans, you have to make plans. If you live alone, and you don't make plans, here is what happens: you wake up ... And it just gets darker.

I caught myself a few weeks ago, clutching my cat to my chest, saying, 'We're all right, aren't we?'

There's no one there taking care of me, there are no rules. I think we need rules, because I'm now watching the least ethical porn. And I don't even know how it happened. I used to say to people – and it was true – 'I can watch pornography as long as the people in it are at least smiling and enjoying what they are doing.' That is not the case any more.

I am now rarely watching anything without a person in it who has been tricked. Everything in my fridge is Fair Trade and organic, the porn is neither.

You just have to make plans right? So you're doing stuff, so life has the illusion of meaning and forward momentum, and that's why you're here, so you've done something tonight. Because tomorrow, people will say, 'What did you do last night?' And you can say, 'I saw a comedy show, because I know things, I'm alive, I'm alive!'

Are you, though? Or are you just desperately filling the time so you don't have to feel all the pain?

Well, you came to the wrong show.

numb

All this loneliness and despair may have been fine if I hadn't been so absurdly sober. Two years earlier I'd visited Thailand, felt a great sense of calm and read a book on Buddhism called *Taming the Monkey Mind*. I didn't think I had the time to become a Buddhist, but not eating other animals or drinking alcohol seemed like a good idea. Alcohol had never been something I liked the taste of anyway and I always assumed everyone else was just pretending.

When I was sixteen, and alcohol was first introduced to my group of friends, I ended up saying, 'This is ridiculous! We're children!'

And then, because I couldn't cope with the peer pressure, I would pretend to be asleep on a sofa, thinking. I can't wait till I'm seventeen, so I can drive away from this fun.

I still don't drink and I understand the reason we drink in this culture ... it creates a fluidity, it means you can cope with the people you love but if you don't have that, you need other coping mechanisms. I've noticed I say the word 'fun' a lot at parties. 'This is fun, this is a fun party, you having fun? I'm having fun! Oh, are you a couple? How long have you been together? How do you keep the spark in your relationship?' And then they feel awkward and I can relax.

numb

But being sober and, underneath everything, still quite shy meant that meeting new people became quite tricky.

I would see somebody at a party that I really liked and I'd think, Gosh, well, he seems just about perfect. Who knows what could happen? I could end up spending the rest of my life with him. And what I would do every time to woo him, to pursue him, to make him see that I was the one for him is I would go home and hope that I saw him again.

I couldn't talk to people. And then I saw the film *Waking Life*. I don't know if you've seen it but one line stood out for me: 'Actual self-awareness is the knowledge that you're a character in someone else's dream.' I love this idea that it could all be a dream and it's somebody else's dream, it makes everything so silly – no need to feel anxious about anything, it's all a dream. And if you're playing a character that isn't serving you – that shy, anxious character that can't talk to people – let go of the character, become a different character.

I was out with a friend of mine, walking through the streets of North London one Sunday afternoon, and during the time that we were together, he took the phone numbers of about four different girls. His thing is that he can go up to girls and say, 'Hello, what's your name?' They exchange phone numbers and then later they have sex. That's a better system than mine.

I said, 'You have to do this for me.'
He then spots this guy that I've been looking
at and before I can run away, scared of what
may occur, he just saunters up to this guy and
says, 'Hello, young man, you look like a fun
chap, what are you up to today in your life?'
And this young student guy says, 'I'm
meeting some friends in the park.'

My friend says, 'Well, we must join
you.' And for some reason this guy doesn't
say, 'why?'

I think it was because my friend said
'we must' and so he just said, 'Oh, well, if
you're in charge of the world, OK.'

We're now sat in this park with
these people and everyone's acting very
nonchalant, like it's normal, but at least in
my head I'm screaming, 'But we're all
strangers!'

I try to chat up the boy I like. I say,
'You look like the cool one in the group',
because I don't know how to talk to humans.
So my friend then rescues me from my
character and says, 'Why don't you two
exchange phone numbers now? We must
move on with our lives!' So we exchange
phone numbers because he's told us to.

Generally in life we feel like we're in control but we're just like ants wandering around hoping to avoid bumping into each other, hoping to avoid doing anything that might embarrass us. But we're not in control of our lives, you're not in control of your lives, half of the people in here are only here because the person next to you likes me.

Maybe more than half. And I'm not in control of my life. I'm not even in control of being here tonight – something happened in my childhood where there was a moment of fear, I responded with something funny and that worked so I carried on with that and now I'm here talking to you, into a microphone, which I don't need because it gives the impression that I'm definitely a stand-up comedian, otherwise I'm just a man standing.

So I asked my friend, 'What do you want me to do now? Shall I text him next week and see what he's up to?'

'No, just text him now and see what he's doing tonight.'

I said, 'That's a bit keen. We just walked away, don't you think I should play hard to get?'

He said, 'No you don't play hard to get, you just picked someone up in a park!'

And he was right, it's this stupid game based on fear, which we don't play in any other area of our lives. In a supermarket you don't think, 'I need some potatoes; oh, I'd better avoid eye contact.' You grab the potato, you bloody eat it and the only difference between a potato and a human being is the fear of rejection, that's the only difference. Everything is a choice between fear and love. We may as well choose love because death is coming. Death is coming. Death is coming.

So I texted him and he was free that night, we were then going on a date, that night . . . I feel like I'm really living some sort of dreamlike existence. My friend then gives me tips on how to have sex with him that evening because this is what life is about. He said, 'Don't talk about the past, don't discuss the future, just keep saying the words "spontaneous" and "adventure" . . .' Spontaneous, adventure, aren't we spontaneous? What an adventure we've been on today. What an adventure it could continue to be. You're spontaneous, I'm spontaneous, when was the last time you decided to be spontaneous? It worked. He taught me two things that day. One, confidence – because why be timid? Death is coming. And two, hypnosis.

do nothing

I learned to say 'yes' to a moment, that there was a way out of my personality. This is also one of the key rules of 'improv' – you mustn't 'block', you have to say 'yes *and* . . .' So if there're two actors in a scene and one of them says, 'Miriam, what are you doing in the castle?', you *mustn't* say, 'This isn't a castle. Who is Miriam?'

However, when I wasn't with my magical friend, I struggled to make anything happen and although I desperately needed love, self-hate refused to help me find it. Loneliness and low self-esteem brought two gifts – I met an actor, so talented, I became incredibly sad that I was a

comedian . . . and a young playwright, who invited
me to such cool parties, I forgot I was funny.

THE COOL PEOPLE

These were very cool people, but they took drugs,
and I don't really take drugs, so that was quite
awkward for me to see that happening in real life,
to see lines of cocaine being racked up on a coffee
table, to be offered a line and to not know what to
say, so end up saying, 'Oh, no thank you, I've just
eaten, you carry on.'

numb

When I was at school they showed us a
video of a girl who took ecstasy and
died. And I thought, Well, I won't do
that, then, I've got a lot to do.

no self

I wasn't cool enough to be at these parties. I was on TV, which meant I had status, but I felt like I shouldn't really have been allowed in. I hadn't written a play or trained at RADA, I was an anxious TV presenter whose only arts qualification was a certificate in preparatory tap.

To describe the people at these parties, there was a guy there called Merlin, and that is not the issue. He, I noticed one night, had the most incredible, perfect, straight white teeth. And I said to him, 'Gosh Merlin! You've got such lovely teeth. Did you wear a brace as a child?!'

'No.' That's the sort of person that was there. They just grew out of his gums without anxiety.

I don't know why there's (still) so much anxiety in my life. The other day, a guy approached me and I wasn't sure if I'd met him before or not. So in the panic of the moment I just said, 'I've got that jumper.' And I didn't.

numb

I'm aware that the anxieties in this book are those of someone whose primary needs have been met but all feelings are valid. Many years ago a therapist told me: if you lost a leg and the person next door lost *two* legs, you would still have lost a leg. I wondered what was going on on this street. And thought it would be best to move, if you could.

There was a lot of talk of Jasper at these parties: 'You must meet Jasper, Simon, he's living in Paris at the moment, but you must meet Jasper.' Jasper arrives six months later and I don't find him attractive, but I don't want to reject another thing at this party, I want to be a guy at the party, I don't want to be the guy sat in the corner, secretly making notes for a show.

I end up saying, 'Maybe we should kiss?'

He then stands up and says, 'I think I might get a drink, actually', leaving me alone . . . thinking I didn't even want him, but he just got back from Paris. That's not a reason to go for someone. Otherwise I may as well be standing at the London terminal for the Eurostar . . . 'Bonjour . . . Oh, Brussels . . . *continue tout droit!*'

I wanted to connect with the people there, I could not. I found out a while ago, Jasper now works for a magazine that comes out twice a year. Why not be really interesting and work for a magazine that doesn't come out? 'Have you read *Toot*?' 'No, no one has; it's too cool for eyes.'

numb

There was a hot tub in the garden where all kinds of things went on. It eventually broke because it was apparently clogged with sin. I would always go home before anything like this happened and even if I had stayed late enough, I don't think I would have had the confidence to take off all my clothes and jump into a hot tub of sin.

The people there were comfortable in their bodies. There were men wearing vests, do you know what I mean? And I, every three or four years, find myself buying a vest, thinking, Maybe this time?

numb

I hated my body when I was a teenager. And then I got to about twenty-five and it became very trendy to be skinny. I got a bit carried away at a party and said, 'I'm quite skinny.'

And a girl said, 'You're not that skinny.' And then I was fat.

numb

I may have developed an eating disorder around this time. I'm not sure if it was an actual eating disorder. I've never deliberately thrown up food, but I did occasionally try much too hard to poo. Is that an eating disorder?

Is it an eating disorder if it includes poking a finger in, to get things going? It's not classic bulimia.

I'm not sure if that paragraph was worth the truth.

The other problem for me at these parties – and it's often a problem when I meet new people – they don't realise that I'm funny.

I was in Shoreditch, in east London recently . . . I was drawn on this particular night to this guy wearing these really big, funny glasses – like really crazy, funny, humorously large glasses – and I said to him, 'Hi, they're big glasses.'

And he said, 'Not really.'

'Small face?'

He said, 'I'm short sighted.'

And I said, 'I know, we're all short sighted but if you can't see how big they are, maybe you need bigger glasses.'

numb

Everything I thought about the people at these parties was a nonsense. They were as young and insecure as I was. In fact, they were younger and possibly more insecure. To cover their anxieties they had alcohol and drugs while I had my personality, which couldn't find a way to be funny around these people and so remained stuck at quiet and sad. At one party we were all stood in the garden watching Chinese paper lanterns floating into the sky. I saw these young, beautiful people cheering and hugging each other and thought, Everyone here is going to age and die.

THE ACTOR

I did fall in love about five years ago but with somebody I invented, which isn't ideal. He was based on somebody who existed but because I had such low self-esteem, I took every negative attribute I felt about myself, converted those into positive attributes and projected those onto him. Thus he would heal me and complete me in my life. Initially, I just liked him because he was really thin. I really like that, like thinner than me, ill thin. I don't know why I like that, I just like the idea I could go on a date with someone and it could be their last date.

I've realised my type is me but better, which I think is OK, I just need to find somebody who wants *himself* but much, much worse.

I went to see him in this play . . . and he was really vulnerable on stage. Weeks had been building up to this moment and all I could manage when I saw him at the party was a kind of polite nod and I don't know if he saw it, he didn't nod back, and then I felt awkward about approaching him at all.

An hour went past and I couldn't approach him and then I saw him leave, I saw him leave the theatre, his rucksack on his back, his little beanie hat on his head, and as he got further and further away, it became harder and harder to move . . . And he was gone. Gone. Three weeks go by of sadness, pain, regret, I've turned him into the only person I can possibly be with in my life.

A lot of it was ego. I just felt like he was going to become a great actor, he could make people cry and I could become a great comedian and make people laugh and if we were together we could be like a two-man Robin Williams. All the talent of Robin Williams but in two separate, thin men.

I didn't know how I was going to meet him again and then I was in a shop in Covent Garden that sells vintage clothing and he was there in the shop. I felt in that moment that God had brought us together. I don't feel that now so much because it feels like the thought of a deluded moron.

I'm not an atheist. I'm a big fan of Jesus Christ, there's nobody more thin and vulnerable than Jesus Christ.

The actor was in that shop at the same time as me and I don't believe in coincidence. Coincidence is a word we invented for something we don't quite understand yet. I read a book called *Illusions: The Adventures of a Reluctant Messiah*. On the cover of this book is a blue feather because the character/author of this book believes in the philosophy 'thinking makes it so, we create our own reality'. He tests this by visualising a blue feather in his fingers, he believes . . . that everything has already been achieved, time is an illusion, so if he feels he has the blue feather already, it will come to him because there is nothing opposing that idea. Later in the book the blue feather appears. I tested this myself with a white feather; I thought I had the white feather in my fingers, not that I needed the white feather or desired the white feather, it had already been achieved. Later I was at a picnic, I put my hand in a packet of crisps, which is something I wouldn't normally do, I pulled out a crisp with a white feather on, which is disgusting.

But there he was in the shop and I don't know how you feel, maybe he walked into that shop at the same time as me with his own legs. No, I put him in that shop with my God mind.

Now some people will say, 'If we do create our own reality, what about the Holocaust, what about things like child abuse, do they create that in their world?' And the thing that you need to understand about that is: 'shh'.

In an ideal world I would have been able to go up to him and just say, 'Hey, how are you? I saw your play the other week, it was great.'

'Oh, thank you, of course, I remember the nod . . . Why are you crying?'

'I have too many sinks.'

Here's what *actually* happened. I saw him there, he hadn't seen me, I was standing about a metre away from him. And what I thought would be really cool and seductive would be to just stand in the middle of the shop, and shout his full name.

He turned round, alarmed – I could see the terror in his eyes – but because I started at a certain volume I thought it would be too odd to get any quieter. So I was then just shouting at him about the good reviews his play had and he says, 'Oh, I don't read reviews.' And he's all timid and vulnerable, which is why I love him!

And I think the difference between us – because I think we were both quite shy as children, I say 'I think', I did a lot of research on him – he retained that shyness and it made him beautiful and sensitive and I decided shyness was something to be overcome . . . He went to a really good acting school in London where he was taught to nourish his sensitivity and nurture his vulnerability and that's what makes him a great actor. I went to a Saturday-morning stage school in Essex where we were taught that whether we were singing, dancing or acting, just do it loud. So I didn't become good at any of those things, but when I danced, people heard.

But now I was in London, talking to this actor and I suggested this club on a Monday night which he hadn't heard of. Which meant that I could say, 'Well, I'll email you the details' – that casual.

He then said, 'OK.' I had his email address, he gave me his email address . . . I went home and composed the most beautiful, funny little email – six friends confirmed it was a beautiful, funny email. I pressed 'send' and this is very much the end of the story. He never emailed back.

do nothing

All this self-hate led me to think that if I couldn't *have* the actor, I would have to become him. I began taking acting lessons, went to see many plays (not all of them starring him) and co-wrote a BBC2 sitcom called *Grandma's House*, in which I played a disillusioned TV presenter seeking a more meaningful life as an actor, as well as the love of a semi-fictional actor.

MUM: Do you want to be with him
or sleep with him?
SIMON: Both, that's normal, isn't it?

GRANDMA'S HOUSE, 2011

At the same time, I continued to stalk the actor, just in case he changed his mind. A friend of mine was in a play upstairs at the Royal Court and he was in the play downstairs, or it could have been the other way round. Downstairs is the bigger space, but as an actor of such integrity, he would have been drawn to the material rather than the size of the room.

I remember exactly what I wore the first time we met again. I went for clothes that I thought he would have worn – a thin green jumper over a lightweight shirt with grey trousers. My hair had never looked so curly or delicious and knowing that I couldn't possibly look any better than I did made his indifference quite tricky to accept.

When both plays were finished, I spotted him in the bar and found the courage to ask him how the play had gone and if he wanted to find somewhere to sit. We found a quiet corner and I then spent the next hour trying to appear to be the most calm, sensitive and connected version of myself that anyone had ever experienced. I was not, in any way, funny. I didn't know how to be, I couldn't tease him about anything because I thought he was perfect. How do you make an angel laugh?

So I spent all my energy trying to appear as pure and mysterious as him. I thought if I could do a really good impression of him, then surely he would like me. Writing this now, I realise he could have had his own self-esteem issues and therefore found meeting himself quite upsetting.

I asked him, as someone so good at acting, if he could give me some acting advice, which was an odd combination of intense flirting and genuine need for advice.

'How does acting work?'

'I don't know,' he said, 'it's just sort of magic', which I found incredibly appealing and totally useless.

I should have remembered what my mum
used to say to me, about how 'you can be or

do anything you want to do in this life
because everyone you see on TV or in films,
they are all shit'. She used to say that a lot.
She would point at the television and say,
'Shit comes out of them; you'll be a star!'

do nothing

Maybe it's difficult *not* to have low self-esteem if
you're born in a Kingdom. I wrote this next bit
of stand-up as a way of expressing how ridiculous
I think it is that we still have a monarchy, but I
think it's really about me feeling like a peasant.

We have a Queen in this country, and not
in *the past*.
    I suppose what's fascinating about
her is she doesn't seem to be
embarrassed! She walks into rooms, there
are trumpets – if that was me I'd say, 'No
you mustn't, it's ridiculous.' But she
stands there, and she thinks, Yes, this
is appropriate.

And then people sing 'God Save the Queen' . . . like she's more important than them . . . If there's going to be a song it should be something like: '[sings] we're all basically the same thing – blood comes out of us and shit and there's sexual fluids and there's phlegm and there's snot . . .' Somebody would have to write it, but that sort of thing.

People love her. I think I preferred it when we thought she'd murdered Diana. I'm really just worried for her, you know, because she's a *person* and there must be so much denial in her life. Every morning she must wake up, do a shit, and for the rest of the day have to pretend that that didn't happen. Because if she accepts that she's just a person who does a shit, those trumpets are going to start to sound sarcastic.

to be free

Meanwhile, the lady teaching me to act must have become frustrated by how defended I was.

I refused to let her in, even though I was paying for the sessions and desperate to be broken down, to be present, to be able to feel something real. She suggested I spend a month at Phillipe Gaulier's clown school in Paris, so I could let go of my inhibitions and free my vulnerable, inner clown.

On the first day, Gaulier asked us to stand up, say our names and what we did for a living. I thought, Well, this is going to go quite well, I'll say, 'I'm Simon and I'm a stand-up comedian.' And he'll say, 'How wonderful, we have a professional in the room.'

Instead, he said in the most appalled French accent, 'Ugh stand-up comedy, so you say a funny thing and everybody thinks it is so funny that you have said something funny, there's nothing more disgusting than stand-up comedy!'

Once the introductions were complete, we spent the whole month performing in exercises designed to strip away context, so that we were forced to be funny in some pure, childlike way. A performer has to have some vulnerability and joy or they stink. Gaulier had a drum and every time he thought someone was being too boring or disgusting he'd bang it and then take a vote on whether anyone would mind if the person on stage was eaten by a shark.

In one exercise, I was paired up with an Australian girl called Tessa. Gaulier said, 'Here is the scene. You are circus performers and the lions have eaten the lion tamer, so there is no lion show today. You have to fill for twenty minutes.'

I wasn't sure what to do but Tessa started saying 'ragghh I am a lion' and jumped around the room. I completely froze. All I could think was, Tessa is *not* a lion.

So I decided to ignore her and announced, 'Ladies and gentlemen, the lions are not available . . .' Gaulier banged his drum. He said, 'No talking!' and I didn't know what else I could do. Tessa carried on being a lion and I couldn't join in. Gaulier banged his drum again and said, 'Tessa, I want you to hit Simon until he is funny.'

I thought, OK, at least this a new scene with some context – Tessa will do some play-fighting and I'll be able to respond in some funny way. But she hit me, hard. I screamed in pain and everyone laughed. I thought, I'm in a lot of pain, but my vulnerability is getting laughs. And then Gaulier banged his drum, and said, 'Very good, but Simon, you know, these laughs are not for you, they are for Tessa's joy in hitting you.'

A few years later, a week after the first series of *Grandma's House* was broadcast on BBC2, I spotted the actor who I'd based one of the characters on, standing outside Sadler's Wells Theatre. Instant terror and excitement. Apparently we'd both booked tickets for the same contemporary dance show on the same night and yet, somehow, we still weren't living together discussing art.

I thought I would casually go up to him and try to bring up the sitcom in a way that suggested I was clearly over him but had used all these ridiculous former feelings to create something beautiful. I wondered how he'd feel about me now. He hadn't been that fussed about me as a TV presenter but now I was a proper comedian, a sort of actor and a writer who had written things about him.

I approached cautiously, said 'hello' in a way that suggested I was someone completely at peace with himself. He said 'hello' in a way that was hard to read.

I said, 'I think I should maybe apologise to you.'

He said, with genuine sensitivity and concern, 'Oh, what for?'

I replied, 'I sort of fictionalised you in something that was just on TV.'

He looked a bit confused and then said, 'Oh, I think I heard about that.'

He'd *heard* about it. He hadn't watched it? I thought, What do I have to do to get your fucking attention?

I actually felt quite good that evening. I was on a date with someone I was really falling for and as we watched the show, I was incredibly happy to be with him, perhaps even happier than I would have ever been with this ethereal actor person.

Six months later, that relationship ended and he went on to write a beautiful album. I listened to it, thinking, I imagine a few of these songs will be about me. None of them. You mustn't date a singer-songwriter. Date a plumber, then you don't know who they're dedicating their piping to.

I want someone to write about me. Why can't someone else write a book connecting all these bits of stand-up and deconstruct who I am? It's so undignified to be sat here doing it myself.

Maybe the worst moment was seeing a photograph of my ex online, hugging the actor who had also rejected me.

I put my hands over my face. I wasn't in the picture. I was sat in my flat alone and there was no way either of them were saying, 'How's Simon?'

A year later, the actor was in another play at the Royal Court. So I thought I'd give myself one more go at making him love me. I felt I'd written and performed all the insanity out of my head and was now ready for something real. I believed this because it would have been unbearable to accept that after all that transformative, healing comedy, I was still the same lunatic.

I found him in the bar and we got talking again. I felt more relaxed than I ever had with him and 1 wasn't pretending this time, I was actually relaxed, though I was also very impressed with how relaxed I was, so I can't have been that relaxed.

We must have sat talking for around an hour, and it was actually a really grounded, relationship-building conversation. The only moment of panic came when he told me that he'd seen a photo of me as a little boy somewhere, which he thought could have been *him*. The sudden lack of distance between us was too much for me. I started ranting about what a brilliant, sensitive child he must have been and what a stage-school maniac I was. He offered me a moment of connection and I couldn't receive it. And then he revealed he was very happy with a boyfriend. A composer. I thought, OK, Simon, we tried our best, he's happy, it's enough now, he's with a composer, we can't beat that. Can he juggle?

He also told me he couldn't email me back all those years ago for reasons more complicated and personal than anything to do with me being less brilliant than him. He *hadn't* rejected me. I put on my coat, we hugged goodbye and I went to the toilet feeling relieved it was over. As I walked out of the toilet, feeling a real sense of completion, he walked in, which I wasn't expecting. We'd had our hug goodbye and I didn't know what else to say, so I said, 'Composer, huh?'

fear of normal

You end up with a relationship, a mortgage, a family . . . So now when people say, 'We're having a baby', I want to say, 'Do you know who else had a baby? Everyone!'

All they're doing is continuing the cycle of misery.

And surely at this time of catastrophic climate change, the least ethical thing you can do is create more human life. Next time someone announces to you the happy news that she's pregnant, spit in her smug, glowing face!

no self

I grew up surrounded by a lot of casually racist, sexist nonsense. My family's general intolerance was completely normal and my anger towards them alerted me to the fact that I wasn't.

I'd watch *Oprah*, where people who said offensive things were booed. I didn't understand how people in Gants Hill were getting away with it but it seemed to be because they were not in front of a studio audience. It confirmed to me that I would only be safe if I got into the television.

Years later, having achieved this, I had a minor meltdown on live radio, which, having thought about it, was possibly about my 'safe space' – showbusiness, a place of endless joy and freedom – suddenly seeming unbearably dull and possibly racist.

At the end of last year, I was promoting my stand-up special numb on the Radio 1 breakfast show. It happened to be the morning of Nelson Mandela's death, which of course was very sad and shocking news. Even though he was ninety-five and human.

I was asked not to make any jokes about it, which confused and upset me because I'm not an insensitive lunatic, I'm a brilliant, vulnerable clown.

On the way to the studio, I walked past the 'urban' music station, 1 Xtra, where I saw black people in a booth (this is not their jingle). Then I arrived at the

Radio 1 studio, which was exclusively white people in a booth.

Nelson Mandela had just died. Black people in one booth, white people in a separate, nicer booth. And I thought, Don't mention that.

The host of the show told me he hadn't written any questions, so opened with a story about a sandwich that he'd eaten. And not even that morning.

He was trying to engage me in this inane small talk so I could come across like a normal, likeable guy but that is not what I'm going for. I want people to hear me on the radio and say, 'Shhh, we must listen for the wisdom', especially on a morning when people are looking for a new spiritual leader.

I was now desperately trying to find something to say to transcend this mundanity. Something thoughtful, inspiring, funny. Then I heard him say 'BBC' and beyond my control, I found myself screaming, 'What's going on at the BBC? There are a lot of white people in here!'

I felt I hadn't made my point that clearly.

So I said, 'Next door there are only black people and I don't think Mandela would approve.' Silence.

The host was forced to read an apology, 'to anyone who found what Simon said offensive'. Off air, the producer told me off and it's very rare that anyone tells me off these days because I'm such a delight.

And the truth is, I don't know what Mandela would have thought about 1 Xtra. He was alive when the station was created, he didn't do anything about it then.

to be free

I really needed laughter in that moment. Laughter would have meant everything was OK but what I said wasn't actually, properly funny, I just panicked and the BBC on the morning of Mandela's death was not a safe space to be almost funny.

And I think this is why I really like people who are autistic. I visited this school that teaches children who are autistic, and I said to the head teacher: 'I don't really know anything, but it seems to me that the child who is autistic doesn't have autism, what they have is a kind of freedom from all the conventions and the nonsense which we have to put up with. And if there's any anxiety which they feel, isn't that often from us trying to make them the same as everyone else?'

And she said: 'Well, that's a nice idea. But sometimes they want to masturbate in public.'

And I think that story's really about me.

It was interesting seeing the social conventions taught at the school, so that a person who is autistic can exist within the culture that we've created. I went to shake this kid's hand and I could see him, as we were shaking hands, thinking, 'This is bullshit, isn't it?'

I was in a classroom where very young kids were being taught to spread jam on toast. And it's not that they

can't physically do that, they just didn't
seem to want to. I could see them looking
around thinking, What are we doing?
This is wasting valuable masturbation
time!

And as I was leaving I walked
through the playground where this
very sweet-looking ten-year-old boy
came towards me. I thought he'd say
hello but he said 'prick' and carried
on walking.

I felt so connected. Because, you
know, what we have in this culture as
appropriate or inappropriate language
is so absurd anyway, that to call somebody
an arsehole is a bad thing to call them?
If we didn't have arseholes we would
explode.

To say to someone, 'you're an
arsehole' is like saying 'you're a vital
member of this community'.

I don't know when the word
'cocksucker' became such an insult. If
there were no cocksuckers, who would
suck all the cocks?

And how can the worst thing you
can call someone be 'cunt'? It is where we

all come from! To say to someone, 'you're a cunt' is like saying 'you're the doorway to life!'

to be free

A few years ago, in an airport on the way home from a comedy festival, I was feeling incredibly free and funny, when I had something similar to the kind of anxiety attack someone who is autistic may have, if something doesn't go how they feel it should.

I was at Dublin airport with a couple of friends, and one of these friends sees this girl that he fancies, working at the MAC make-up counter, finds her very attractive, won't stop talking about her, so I say 'well, let's go and say hello', because we're alive.

So, we get to the make-up counter, and I think it has been my idea so I should probably host the flirting, so I say, 'Hello! What's all this?'

She tells us about the new MAC range

that's available and in order to get my friend involved with her, in a flirty silly way, I ask, 'What would you recommend for my friend with his pale skin? What would you recommend for him?'

She says, 'Well, your girlfriend—'

'Oh no, there's no girlfriend,' I say, 'he's very much single. What would you recommend for him?'

She says, 'Well, if you had a girlfriend—'

'No!' I say. 'There's no girlfriend! What would you recommend for *him*?'

She says, 'Well, women . . .'

And then, I don't know why, but I was warm from fury.

We all combine the male and the female . . . It upsets me to hear trendy young couples saying things like, 'We're having a baby, we don't know the gender yet, so we don't know whether to paint the nursery blue or pink. We might go for yellow just to be safe.' Safe? What's the danger? Go blue, go nuts! 'But what's if it's a girl? We don't want her to grow up to be Bruce Willis!'

I start saying things like, 'What if Eddie Izzard walked up to you, this is very limiting!' She didn't know who he was, which annoyed me.

She was beautiful and she knew that she was beautiful but I think that's all she knew. And that is only jealousy, because if you're beautiful that is all you need. I used to get so excited by models at parties, these models, got to have the models, I want a model! And then I was at a party, there were two models in front of me, I was all ready to go into action, and I thought, Oh fuck you. Because what have they done? They've grown high! I learned to juggle.

She was wearing a lot of make-up but we can't judge her for that. She works at the make-up counter, the hours go by, she gets bored, these things can accumulate.

I think that's a problem quite specific to the make-up counter, it's very rare to go into a shoe shop, and somebody's covered in shoes.

I'm screaming and sweating . . . people are looking, I don't even care, it's all beyond my control now. My other friend comes over and says, 'Is everything all right?'

And I say, 'No! We want to buy some make-up! But apparently we should just fuck off!'

And then I see my first friend who is clearly thinking, Well, this isn't quite what we planned.

numb

The worry is that incidents like this could still happen. I occasionally feel incredibly threatened by the conventional. I went to a wedding recently that was just a little too white, heterosexual and Christian. I had an intense feeling that if the Nazis came and took me away, the people at the wedding would feel sad but not stop them.

I can't believe people still get married, people with degrees. These couples have usually already lived together for ten years. What is this wedding for? Two people who are already living together wish to announce they are to continue as they are. A couple who are apparently already happy. Why not just stay in your house and shush? Send an email saying, 'We've been together for ten years, it's going well, carry on.'

It should be the single people sending out invitations saying, 'I'm so lonely, can we *please* have one day where I don't feel sad?'

What would be wrong with this conversation?

`I love you.´

`I love you too.´

`Should we put on a big event to tell everyone we know?´

`Seems arrogant.´

It's at least a little boastful, isn't it? You wouldn't get everyone together to announce, 'We've made lots of money and we think it will last until death.'

A few years ago, a friend told me, 'I'm marrying my girlfriend; it's just getting to that point where we either get married or split up.' How can you either be about to stay together until one of you dies or never see each other again?

And we made it all up – marriage, it's not a naturally occurring thing. We had to have all this romantic language – 'will you marry me?' – because it couldn't be the truth, which is 'will you please save me from my loneliness and depression?', because people would have said, 'I'm quite busy.'

numb

We're all stuck in this prison of appropriate behaviour. I went to see a student play recently – nineteen-,twenty-year-old students on the stage and I was sat next to two fifty-year-old women. One of them was the mother of one of the kids in the play and the other one said to her, 'Gosh, your Timothy has turned out to be quite a stud, hasn't he?' She said it in quite a light, innocent way but I sensed what she was saying there was, 'I'd like to fuck your son.' And I thought, What kind of society is this, where she can't just say that?

to be free

I find myself so impatient for this time that we are in, the things that we consider acceptable, normal ... People talk about the past, history like *that* was all ridiculous – 'how could any of that have happened?' I would like to be in the future *now*, so I could look back at this time and say things like: Do you remember when people got upset when their pets died? And then when other animals died they *ate* them? Do you remember when people drank milk from other species? Did they see cows feeding their calves and think, Yeah, that's probably for me. Do you remember when people felt proud to be British? It's just where you happened to fall out of your mother's vagina. 'I'm so proud to be British' ... You may as well be proud to be caesarean.

All these flags everywhere ... If you're going to have a flag, have a picture of a vagina on the flag, so then you can say, 'Hello, this is where I come from; where do you come from? Oh, the same place, let's be friends.'

How was peace finally achieved? The introduction of the vagina flag.

numb

This fear of normal isn't just an abstract idea. I was circumcised by people who weren't even religious – 'We've had a boy, we'd better cut off a bit of his penis, otherwise people will think we're weird parents.' The buffet wasn't kosher, 'oh no we don't care about that bit, we just love the cock cutting!'

Around a year ago, I was feeling a little lost and ended up at a retreat where a group of people led by a shaman took part in a series of sweat lodges, a Native American ritual for resolving conflict within a warm, womb-like teepee, in Norfolk.

The idea seemed to be to sweat and chant all the conflict out of you and then crawl out of the womb-like teepee, reborn. I experienced the first sweat lodge 'ceremony' mainly as an observer. I didn't really understand what was going on or why it had to be so hot.

In the second sweat lodge, a conflict of gender equality arose. The shaman had explained that women were not allowed in if they were on their 'moon period'. This is what the shaman called a 'period'.

One of the women on this retreat, who was on her moon period, snuck in. And the shaman somehow knew. He began to provoke the women in the group, taking on a not so subtle chauvinist character, creating a lot of stress in what was already quite a hot teepee.

I had a sense that this patriarchal

dominance was what I would have experienced
in the womb, and now felt I could maybe hold
the key to resolving sexism.

I don't understand how we can be sexist. I
mean, apart from the fact that there are
so many women, you'd think it would
be rude.

It's where we all come from.
When do we begin to be sexist? Are we
there in the womb thinking, Well, this is
all very well but I think my dad would
do a better job than this hysterical
witch!

Women. You control the
continuation of human existence. Until
there is equality, you should stop
breeding. I mean, have a baby if you want
to have a baby but if it's a boy, you must
abort. Yes! Because it's a war – if you're a
woman having sex with a man and
creating more men, you should be hung
for treason. Do you think Winston
Churchill would have got pregnant

knowing there was a fifty-fifty chance he
could have a Nazi?

Some of these are new thoughts.

to be free

In the first sweat lodge ceremony I'd said
something funny and felt pleased to have got a
big laugh but then wondered why I was trying to
get laughs in a sweat lodge.

This time, I found myself really wanting
to speak but embarrassed by the sincerity of it
all. The tension between the men and women
was by now unbearable. The men didn't know
what to say about the 'moon period' situation,
many of the women started talking about how
they'd been treated in the past by men and the
shaman's girlfriend started crying. Then my
hands, followed by my entire body, began to
vibrate. Something needed to come out of me. I
finally said, with total conviction, 'I would like to
honour my mother for doing her best under
difficult circumstances.' That was all I planned
to say but then, this rushed its way out of me:

'. . . And I would like to honour my gay child self for doing the same.'

The shaman looked at me approvingly, like an older gay brother who understood my entire journey and also like a heterosexual shaman who'd been waiting for a gay baby to resolve this gender conflict. I felt strong, ready to be reborn, but I wanted to protect my child self before he was birthed into Essex. I thought about my mother who would not be the powerful resource I would need her to be in the conflicts that would follow. I knew I would find strong women in the television. I thought about Roseanne, Ruby Wax, French and Saunders, Oprah Winfrey, and then I covered myself in mud. Nobody else was doing this. I needed to have this baby protected and now with my mud and my TV women, I crawled out of the 'womb' and lay down on the grass. I burst into tears and looking up at the men and women who'd come over to thank me for what I'd said, thought, I did resolve sexism, what a brilliant baby.

daddy

> ... we didn't talk for a while and then my dad
> phoned me and said, 'One day I'm going to be on
> my deathbed and if we don't have a relationship,
> there'll be regret.' So now we see each other once
> a month, which isn't much fun, but when he dies,
> I'm going to feel pretty great.

numb

When I was twenty-three, I went to my dad's second wedding, full of tightly repressed rage, only given expression by my wedding outfit. I wore a suit because it was a wedding but I also went for a bright red T-shirt with the word 'ANTI' printed on it, a necklace with a silver gun pendant and a brooch that looked a bit like a swastika. 'OK, Dad, I'll come to your wedding but only if I can come dressed as anger.'

When I was twenty-five, my friend Kevin told me about something called The Landmark Forum – a three-day, life-transforming course. Around 150 people in a room in Euston, were encouraged by the 'leader' to phone people 'who you've been blaming for everything in your lives'. I phoned my father and said, 'Hi, I think I've been ... I'm sorry for blaming you for the divorce that happened. I think I understand now that you were a fallible human being, and not the evil monster that I made you out to be at the time.'

He said, 'I've been waiting ten years to hear that.' It felt like a real moment of healing. And then he said, 'What else did you learn at this course? Did they tell you it's possible the divorce made you gay?'

I said, 'Shush, we just sorted everything out!'

Maybe I'm holding on to this anger for my father, so I don't have to deal with the anger I have for my mother ... who I've idealised in the past when the truth is I had a memory of her in a very stressful moment, I guess, telling me and my siblings, 'One day you'll come home from school and I'll be gone!'

I reminded her of this recently and she said, 'I don't remember that but I was a single parent.'

      I said, 'That's worse, one had already gone!'

to be free

I called my mum during the course, unsure what to say to her but certain I should call to resolve *something*. I said, 'I don't blame you for the divorce,' and she said, 'Of course you don't. It was your father's fault.'

      She then told me that my dad wasn't very good during the pregnancy. A friend of hers, called Marc, took her to the zoo one day. He was apparently very sweet and kind to her. She thought about raising me with him instead. She said, 'I decided to stay with your father but that's why your middle name is Marc.'

      I convinced my mum to come to the course, to see if she'd sign up. She thought I'd joined a cult. My dad had no interest in attending.

      Marc would have come.

My father came over to my flat recently. I'd just been dumped by perhaps the first person I had ever loved. In the same week of this happening, my washing machine broke. My father came over to fix the washing machine and I thought, Perhaps in this moment, we could actually talk about something, he could be my father, provide some wisdom, nurture me in some way. He did not have the capacity to discuss a break-up; he could fix the washing machine. I felt very angry that day that that is what happened. And I've since come to the realisation that he did what he could do, and that's the love. So now when people say to me, 'That's a nice shirt, Simon, is it new?' No. My father loves me.

. . . My childhood perception of him is very different to what it is now. He dealt with a family crisis recently in such a beautiful, calm way. And my memory of him is that he was mostly angry and distant.

I said to him afterwards, 'Who are you? How did you do that?'

And he said – this is what he actually said to me – 'About two years ago, I cut out wheat.'

I could have had a happy childhood. Instead of 'Where's Daddy?' – 'Oh, he'll be back soon; he's just eaten a lot of pasta.'

numb

My dad didn't take up the invitation to see either of my last two stand-up shows. He told me it wasn't his sort of thing and that I didn't need his validation any more. I tried not to be hurt. I'm not into darts but if I had a son who played professional darts and was receiving wonderful reviews, I'd watch him play darts, wouldn't I?

Despite my father's lack of attendance, I used to see him in the audience anyway. Every time I spotted a man who wasn't laughing, I'd feel my father's indifference and say things like, 'Do you think you'll laugh at any point or carry on with *this* face?' If a man ever left to go to the toilet, I'd scream, 'Where are you going? How funny do I have to be, Daddy?'

In the end, I thought, Do I really need my father's love? Can't I just love myself at this point and be grateful to the strangers who love me as long as I'm funny?

I realised eventually that the problem was my expectation of this man as a 'father'. I thought, Let's stop thinking of him as my 'father' and start thinking of him as 'the man who ejaculated'. He ejaculated and so I'm alive, what more do I want? And often when men have ejaculated they are tired, you can't expect them to love you. I can't keep shouting for the rest of my life, 'If you can't love a child, don't ejaculate in a wife, do it out the window!'

If I'm to focus on anything, it should be on thanking my mother for birthing me out of her own body. How can I ever thank her for that? The best I can do is occasionally introduce her to a celebrity. 'Thank you for your womb, here's Derren Brown.'

I'd let go of the idea of my father as my father but then someone said, 'But he's your father', and I felt something. So we met up and he told me he'd just trained to be a hypnotherapist. In my head, I screamed, *What? You can't be the healer, you're the trauma!*

He then said he just needed some clients to get started. What he'd love was for my 'crazy friends' to come to him so he could be a 'hypnotherapist to the stars'. I said nothing. Because why tell someone how you feel at the time, when you could save it up for a book and invite them to a launch that won't be their sort of thing?

Yet through this hypnotherapy training, my father seemed to have developed a language for expressing more emotions than I'd witnessed in him before. We spoke about *his* childhood. He told me he had a very cold, distant mother, which must be worse than having a distant father. So it turned out *he* was the more vulnerable one and I had to love *him*. How did he turn it around? I realised I could no longer feel hostile to this sneaky little hypnotist.

Yet I'd also come to a place where there was a mild sadness but an acceptance of the fact that we didn't really have a relationship. I finally knew in my body that *he* wasn't going to become a different person. I forgave him but didn't necessarily need to see him, which I think is a valid position to hold.

And then my mum called me, very upset because I hadn't been invited to his daughter's (my half-sister's) bat mitzvah, on account of having a boyfriend who is a boy. In the Jewish religion, if you're a boy and you have a boyfriend, it's important that he's a girl.

That line is straight out of the Torah.

I said to my mum, 'Of course we haven't been invited. It's fine, he's not a monster; he just has a religion without which he can't cope. You can't be angry; he's a man with special needs.

Having said that out loud, I felt like I'd finally shifted all the rage. I was over any need for my father's acceptance, validation or attention. I was at peace. And then, the next evening, I received an email inviting my boyfriend and I to the bat mitzvah. I was furious.

All that work to accept that he would never change and then he changed? I tried everything to make him be OK with me. How dare *he* decide the fight is over.

I called him a few days after the email. Following some polite chit-chat I cautiously said, 'So, you've had a bit of a change of heart?'

He said, 'Not really.'

I said, 'Something happened, no?'

He said, 'Listen, let's say you were in St John's Wood and you wanted me to drive you to Edgware,' which already made no sense.

He continued, '. . . and on the drive you fell asleep, then when you woke up, you were exactly where you wanted to be, would it matter how we got there?'

I thought about this. Does it matter how we've got here? I said, 'Hang on, I haven't been *asleep* for twenty years!' And then, because I was scared I wouldn't be able to stop shouting at him if I started, I said, 'You know, feelings have been felt.'

He said, 'I understand.' And I decided to hear, 'I'm sorry', because often it's best to make up the words you need to hear, like when he said

'You don't need my validation any more', I could have heard, 'I couldn't be more proud of you'.

He also suggested this had all been good material for me, which was difficult to argue with.

My father says, 'Why don't you bring along some of those magic tricks you used to do, and then you can entertain all the children,' because when I was – I wish this was younger – seventeen . . . Because no one ever said to me, 'It's nice, Simon, that you do magic, you might like sex.'

So I had no sex until I was twenty-one and I really feel like I had to make up for lost time, so there's been quite a bit of sex, but I very much miss the magic.

numb

My boyfriend and I went to the bat mitzvah. In contrast to the tension I felt at his wedding, I felt incredibly peaceful. As I walked in I could see how vulnerable my dad was. It must have been quite scary for him, having us there. One of the first people I saw was a woman who, years before, had tried to convert me to Orthodox Judaism. When I told her I didn't think it was for me, she said, 'But are you happy?' And I *wasn't* happy, so I thought, Oh she's got me.

Seeing this woman again, I thought, I'm happy now.

She said, 'It's been a long time. Are you married?'

I gestured to my boyfriend and said, 'No, I've been with this guy for five years.'

She looked nervous and I could have left her hanging but I filled the space by telling her how great he was. She said, 'OK, I guess that's OK.'

I agreed that it was OK and then she walked away. I thought, Yes, I killed her with love.

Then a rabbi came over and I took a deep breath. I asked him what he gets up to when he's not hosting bat mitzvahs. He said he also does weddings and suggested he could do my wedding. I was about to say, 'Oh, well, you won't because, you *won't*.' But instead, I just smiled.

He asked if I was married already and I pointed towards my boyfriend again. The rabbi didn't know what to say, so he hugged me. In the hug, I went from feeling alarmed to patronised to realising that he wasn't hugging me, I was hugging a child who had just heard something that had scared him.

. . . it feels like an unkind thing to do, to attack religious people, It just feels rude. If you're at a party and you get into a conversation with someone who says, 'Oh, I'm a Christian or I'm a Muslim or I'm a Jew', it's very rude to say, 'Oh how ridiculous!'

I feel at this point we have to treat people with kindness, love and respect in the same way you treat a child running around the party saying, 'I'm a helicopter.' Good for you, we're all having fun; I'm a choo-choo train.

do nothing

There is a calm now to my relationship with my father. We stopped wanting to fix each other. And I've accepted that everything that happened couldn't have been any different. If it had been, I'd be an entirely different person so to want to alter the past would only be another form of self-hate.

The key story I have for remembering that my father is just a fallible man is this one: When I was ten, my mum was pregnant for the fourth time. I was about to have a sister, so a wife. 'When's my wife due, Mummy?'

At the time, our two pet rabbits had just had five of their own babies. My mum was concerned that there would soon be a human baby crawling around the garden and didn't want there to be rabbit droppings everywhere. So she asked my dad to re-home the rabbits. How would he do this? My father took my seven-year-old brother and me to the local park and set the rabbits free. A dog came. We watched as the dog chased and mauled at least two of the smallest rabbits. My brother cried. I kept it all inside, where it stayed for twenty years. And when I think of the baby rabbits, I know that if they'd been looking up at my father, desperately searching for an explanation or an apology, they would only have suffered more. Better for the baby rabbits to think, This is just a man who doesn't know what he's doing.

saving the boy

I remember when I was turning thirty a couple of years ago, I had a crisis. I didn't know there was going to be a crisis until this moment in my life – I was wandering along a street, in some skinny jeans, trainers and a yellow hoody. I saw a reflection of myself in a shop window and thought, Does my head look too old for these clothes?

And I could not concentrate on anything else that day because I thought, Everything in my life depends on youth. My personality is cheeky, you have to be young for cheeky – 'oh young Simon he's so funny and cheeky'. Uncle Simon is creepy.

And Grandpa Simon, he's in prison.

numb

At twenty-nine I began what would be two years of psychotherapy. I thought it would be fine to be thirty as long as I became a different person.

I often feel like this must be a temporary personality before I get to the good one. Surely this can't be it for life. This voice, this is my voice!

And I have this laugh now, and I don't know when it started but this is my actual laugh – 'Ha!' I can't experience prolonged joy.

numb

I was lonely and only ever attracted to vulnerable, young, men. The psychotherapist told me I had classic depression, which I was not happy about. I didn't mind having depression but I would have preferred not to have the standard version. I didn't think I was depressed, I thought I was profound.

. . . life is cyclical and repetitive, do you know what I was thinking about when I was in the toilet the other morning? Again? It's always the same, isn't it? Once, about six years ago, I had a green shit, once. And it looked at me as if to say, Perhaps everything will be different now.

do nothing

I'd just left another therapist who told me, 'You're a claustrophobic narcissist and would benefit from group therapy.' I found group therapy quite interesting, in that I like being the new person in a group and love hearing people talk so openly. Someone expressed some upset about no longer being the youngest person in the group, which made me feel young again. A man in his early fifties spoke about having a new stepson who didn't like him and how the mother always sided with her son. Everyone was nodding and I was sat there thinking, She *should* side with the son, who the hell are you? You're not my real dad!

I could see how this group situation could be transformative for everyone involved but noticed after a few weeks that nothing seemed to be happening. I saw *some* progress – a woman who'd been sat slumped on a sofa each week suddenly sat up and was feeling better, but a week later went back to slumped.

I asked why she was lying on the sofa again and she responded, 'I don't know, why do you laugh like that?'

About a month after I left the group, the therapist, whose aim was to cure me of narcissism, emailed to say that she was writing a book about group therapy and wondered if it was OK to include a chapter she had written about me called 'The Unsuitable Patient'.

An old school friend told me that I just think too much, which was valid but he then very boastfully said to me, 'You know, I *never* think.'

I said, 'You do, you do think.'

And he said, 'Nope.'

I said, 'Look, even if you're not discussing philosophy every moment of your life, you'll have come to some conclusions, like when you wake up and you get out of bed, why do you do that?'

And he said, 'I've got work.'

And then I got annoyed and said, 'Well, why don't you just kill yourself?'

And then my other friend leaned in and said, 'He seems quite happy, don't ruin another life.'

numb

I feel special in some way if I feel broken. If I'm broken, there's a journey to be fixed. In the meaninglessness of it all, I feel unique, I feel special.

I like the fact that I have an osteopath appointment once a month where I go because I have bad posture – something happened in my past and I guess this man is healing me, bringing me to some sort of pure, neutral state.

I asked him (because he's quite a sensitive sweet man), 'Why did I end up with bad posture? Is it because when I was a kid I was quite shy and I wanted to make myself invisible so I ended up all hunched over and scared? And even though I do what I do now, still inside, I'm the same scared crying child, what's wrong with me, what's wrong with me?'

And he said, 'You have very tight hamstrings.'

'Yeah but isn't it more that I'm a genius recluse?'

'No, the tendons behind your knees are rather restrictive.'

'But isn't that just the physical manifestation of a tortured soul?'

'No, it's your legs.'

do nothing

My new therapist, who was happy to provide one-on-one sessions, explained how they would work. I wasn't sure what to say so I said, 'OK, fun.'

She looked at me, concerned, and said, 'It isn't fun.'

In our second session, I was being quite funny and she suddenly said, 'It's really great that you can be funny but you don't need to be funny in this room.'

I understood what she was saying and carried on talking until she interrupted again, 'You know, you don't have to be interesting.'

I was confused and asked, 'Do you want me to tell these stories but not as well?'

She wanted me to cry. She wanted a real emotional connection in the room, so I could express some emotions in a relationship outside the room. She wanted me to be authentic and grounded, which I found quite tricky because I was so funny and interesting.

Often we'd sit in silence. Even though I understood everything we discussed was confidential, I knew that *I* would definitely end up writing about it. She told me I could decide later if what we spoke about would end up on stage and assured me that not *everything* had to be made public. It took me a while to accept this.

Eventually we discussed age.

'What if I age?'

'Well, you will.'

'I don't want to.'

I didn't know why ageing was such a problem for me. It wasn't that if you age too much you end up dead, I was fine with death. It was getting older that terrified me – getting older and not dying.

I was at the theatre and I saw somebody who turned out to be eighteen. And he was with a woman who turned out to be his mother.

But she, it turned out, was a fan of mine. She likes my work; I like her son, great. Also, I've worked really hard since about the age of thirteen to get to wherever the hell I am today, so if she's taken any enjoyment from my work, I think I've earned her child.

We get talking and they are delightfully uber middle class. And I'm from Essex so this feels like a moment where I've arrived . . . After the play, I end up sat on the steps of this theatre with just him. It's about 11.30 in the evening, there's romance in the air and then his mother comes round the corner and I feel awkward. I think, Oh gosh, the mother must love him and will be protective of him. But she says, 'OK, goodbye darling, see you later.' Leaves me with her son, so I thought, Oh, she's given him to me. So I took him.

He took me to this restaurant that he knew, it was his area . . . We spoke for two hours – he was actually much more mature than you'd imagine for eighteen, much more intelligent that you'd imagine for eighteen and all those other things that people like me say.

We started meeting up for these kind of dates, not defined as such but they were dates. Eventually, I invited him back to my flat. I wasn't sure if it would be a bit much for him and I'm not very good at making the first move but I thought I would have to because I'm the responsible adult here.

I couldn't quite make the move, there was just something so awkward about it and it was awkward for him as well because he's straight, so it's difficult.

But everything is seemingly leading towards this kiss, we're edging closer to each other on the sofa . . . And at one point I thought I *had* to kiss him because I found myself fiddling with his hair and thought, I have to do the kiss now because that's a precursor to a kiss. If you don't then do the kiss, you're a weirdo who just likes hair. 'Well, it's been lovely touching your hair this evening, let yourself out.'

So I leaned in, kissed him on the lips and said, 'I've just kissed you on the lips, is that OK?'

He said, 'Yeah, it's fine, it's fine . . .'

So I kissed him again and said, 'I've just kissed you on the lips again,' because kids love repetition.

And actually it was a really lovely experience for both of us, I don't feel any shame or regret about it . . . Now I . . . Look, it's not ideal being with an eighteen-year-old but there's nothing we can do about the fact

he was eighteen, there's nothing we can do
about the fact that if I'd met him five
weeks before, he would have been
seventeen. Nothing *we* can do, nothing the
police can do, no one can do anything.

do nothing

I realise now that my panic about getting older, much more than vanity, was about ending up further away from my teenage self. When I was eighteen, it seemed impossible to just accept who I was and have some fun with another eighteen-year-old. And this was one of the key revelations from therapy – I kept being drawn to these young, vulnerable men in an attempt to save the eighteen-year-old in me, who wasn't saved. You may prefer to think of me as a pervert ... but that is an official medical diagnosis.

Around the same time, I met a skinny boy with big, curly hair, at a party in Amsterdam.

I was in Amsterdam for about three days, thinking about sex just the whole time that I was there apart from, I don't know, forty minutes in the Anne Frank museum? And I was there for an hour.

numb

He was talking to a much older man and looked like he needed to be rescued by a slightly less older man. He was incredibly cute. He told me about his depression, anxiety, his inability to sleep, I was really turned on. I told him about a guided mediation series that I'd found helpful. We went back to my hotel room and it occurred to me that I had this meditation series with me. So I gave him my headphones and said, 'I'm going to the toilet, but have a listen to this!' When I walked out of the bathroom, he was asleep. Apparently my need to save him was greater than my desire to do anything else. Or his need for sleep was greater than his desire for me.

I didn't know why I kept going for the same sort of weird, vulnerable, quiet sort of person and then I realised it comes directly from being about fifteen years old and watching the drama *My So-Called Life* starring Jared Leto as Jordan Catalano.

Everyone I've ever gone for has been some version of Jordan Catalano. I watched the DVD to see what it was about this character and figured it was these three things: Number One – He has about four lines in every episode.

Number Two – He has long hair that sometimes falls over an eye and he'll tuck it behind his ear. Which is amazing, isn't it? It's just amazing.

And the third thing is he is dyslexic.

And that's all I've ever wanted – a near mute with long hair and learning difficulties.

And there's nothing wrong with any of those things, I don't want to offend anyone, if that describes you in any way, I'd like to meet you.

Recently, I went to see a play in which there was an actor . . . I knew the playwright and we went to eat after the play. I was sat next to the actor that I fancied. I was talking to him about how we live in a culture where you can order stuff online and it comes within the next day or two. We live like that now and so it's frustrating to not be able to order a specific human being from the universe and have them come towards you. He said, 'Well, what do you want? Who do you want?'

I say – and I hadn't thought about this for a while – I say, 'I want Jared Leto.'

He then says, in that moment, 'I just did a film with Jared Leto where I played the younger version of his character.'

I didn't know what to do with that. I'd only just ordered him.

He then says out of his mouth, 'Do you want to see a sex scene I did as the young Jared Leto?'

I say, 'Yes.' And it's so close to the fantasy, it's even closer to the fantasy than the actual Jared Leto in real life now. Who oddly I did meet about three years ago in Thailand at a full moon party. I didn't realise it was him, I just thought it was someone who looked like him. So I went up to him and said, 'You look a lot like Jared Leto. Do you know who Jared Leto is?'

He said, 'I *am* Jared Leto.'

I wasn't ready for that.

So all I could manage to say was, 'Your beauty in *Requiem for a Dream* detracted from the narrative.'

He thanked me and walked away.

do nothing

I'm still friends with the young Jared Leto. He's incredibly beautiful and that's possibly why he's my friend. He's very funny as well but if he didn't have his face and hair, I think we'd do a lot more on email. I thought I was over any attraction to him recently and then he took his hat off and his hair (despite having been in a hat) was still incredible. If I put a hat on and then took it off, I'd have to go home.

Beauty is too powerful. I feel mildly better now but I used to see pretty boys and just feel tired. I'd see someone and think, Oh great, now I have to think about *you* for ten years!

I really enjoy spending time with him but there's always this terrible regret that hangs over me, that I should have kissed him, that there was this moment when I could have but I was too sad and confused. We had just inhaled some nitrous oxide from balloons . . .

... because I don't do drugs, but I will if they come in balloons.

numb

I fell back on the bed we were sat on, with my arms splayed apart. He then fell back, his head landing in my arm. He said, 'This is the most erotic moment of my life . . .' And because of self-hate, I thought, He's probably said the wrong word. He probably means erratic? Or asthmatic?

At thirty-one, I found the ultimate, vulnerable, young 'me' – curly hair, depression, glasses, he had it all. I wanted to ask him to move in with me and never leave. He didn't move in and then he left.

I tried so hard to make him happy. He once looked directly at me and said, 'When you try to be funny or positive, it doesn't help.' I thought, That's all I've got.

It took a long time to even create a relationship, to make it a thing. He wanted something more casual and I really wanted something real at that point in my life. We had this whole discussion one night – he said to me, 'Look, maybe I don't want to be Simon Amstell's boyfriend,' which was really hard for me to hear because I *am* Simon Amstell.

Everything went well for about six months, and then he started this job, which meant we weren't seeing each other enough. And it all became very tense because I didn't know whether us not seeing each other was about the job or about us. I thought if I just put some dates in my diary, there would be stuff to look forward to and everything would be fine.

We meet up in a park square and we sit on a bench. He says to me, 'I can't be in this relationship any more.' 'Can't' was the word. *Can't!* And I thought, You *could*, I've brought my diary.

He doesn't want to discuss it; he's not in a place where he can talk about it. So we hug, and we part, I feel all confused, I feel like I may cry but I can't in the middle of this park square. So I see a coffee shop in the distance and I think, I will go into their toilet and cry in the coffee shop toilet, which I was concerned about because often they don't let you cry unless you purchase something first.

So I'm walking to the coffee shop, there's all this build-up of emotion, I get to the toilet, I shut the door behind me and I'm so emotionally blocked that I feel one tear come ... And I'm so pleased that's happened, I stop crying.

I arrive home and this is the hardest part for me – I can't feel any of the pain, I go straight to my computer and start typing up what's happened, so I can tell *you* about it! And I'm annoyed with my own fingers for typing – Why do we have to do this so soon? Because we're too talented!

numb

I felt sad for a long time after that. I really loved him and thought about him constantly. Once it was over, I remember meeting someone similar at a party – skinny, funny, pretty, I think he may have even fancied me – and I just couldn't be bothered. Something is very wrong if you meet someone you like and your body says, 'What for?'

I met up with my ex a while ago to discuss what had actually happened. And one of the things he said was that *I* was vulnerable and I needed someone to take care of *me*.

This did not ring true, because I'd always taken care of myself.

But then, I was in a spa hotel in Spain, because life lessons can come from anywhere – many will come tonight. You won't realise, you'll think you've seen a comedy show and then tomorrow you'll think, Perhaps I should leave my husband.

I was going to have this massage but it suddenly wasn't available, so the lady in charge asked if I wanted another massage, which I hadn't heard of, and also this flotation tank treatment, which intrigued me. I said yes to both because I had time and I thought that they would be two separate events. What it turned out to be was me lying back in warm water, in a dark room with a man swinging me about.

And I loved it.

It was this magical, warm, womb-like space and he was everything, he was my mother, father, brother, lover – and also relieving neck and shoulder pain wonderfully.

Bizarrely for this womb-like situation, I found him quite attractive in there. And he wasn't my usual type, he was quite muscly. I normally go for someone who has no muscles, no bottom, just a stick and a head.

This guy, not only did he have this strong body, he also had a very kind, vulnerable face, and that's a good combination for me – a swimmer's body, but the face of someone who maybe can't even swim.

His body was saying, 'I will protect you in this room'; his face was saying, 'I could drown.' And as he's massaging my shoulders, moving me in the water, in the darkness, I feel his breath on my face. And I think, Perhaps there are no consequences in the womb, and I could just lean up and kiss him. But I couldn't do that, because even in that dreamlike, womb-like space, fear was still present, and I was so annoyed at my own fear . . . But then I told this story to a friend, who said, 'It's good that fear was present, that would have been really odd.'

So I didn't do that but when he got out of the water and told me to get dressed when I was ready, I ended up saying in a panic because I felt like this man who had been nurturing me, healing me, was about to leave, 'Are you sure you don't want to get back in?' Like a crazed middle-aged housewife. 'Please! My husband won't touch me!'

numb

Around this time, I had been on two stand-up tours – *no self* and *do nothing* – with my friend and occasional support act Arnab Chanda.

The first time we played Oxford, we bumped into a group of young men on the street after the show. I don't think they'd been in the audience but they were walking past the stage door as we came out. We got talking and then went to see a band playing nearby.

I of course fancied one of them – Freddie – and we began talking in the bar of the music venue about his various issues. The whole group ended up at our hotel bar. His brother told me he thought that Freddie was gay but hadn't figured it out yet and asked if I would help. I said I'd try my best.

We ended up in my room, sat on the bed. Freddie said that he felt he should tell me that he was straight and was worried he'd led me on. So we spoke for about two hours, on a bed. I liked speaking to him. I really wanted to kiss him. He said he didn't want me to feel like he was only in there because of who I was and I didn't want him to feel he was only there because I wanted to sleep with him so we were a bit stuck.

There was a lot of moving around the room. As he smoked out of the window, I was becoming more and more exhausted, trying to figure out what this actually was. Was he interested? Lonely? More lonely than me? Confused? More confused than me? He told me he'd been with boys before but wasn't sure if he was into it. I said, 'Right, yeah, it's tricky.'

I feel a bit horrified by this story now. I just wanted to feel something other than lonely. He may have wanted a friend more than he wanted sex. I listened to him, gave some advice, but I guess it wasn't very pure as I wanted sex more than I wanted a friend. Why couldn't it have been both, Simon?

I was feeling like I should be assertive and take a risk. I said something like, 'Maybe I should just kiss you and see how that goes.' I went to kiss him and he pulled away. I thought, OK, this all feels a bit humiliating now and I said I was tired. He looked guilty. He said he shouldn't have come to the room. I said it was all fine, it had been fun and I just needed to sleep. We hugged goodbye. Mid hug, to cover my frustration and shame, I made a stupid joke about how he should probably go before he gets an erection. He half smiled and I apologised for the joke. Before he left he said he'd like to see me in London. I said 'sure' and closed the door.

I collapsed on the bed and said to myself, Oh my God, what am I doing? What do I have to do?

When he came to London, he texted me. I responded, 'Have you figured out who you are yet?', which was a bit aggressive but I thought I couldn't keep chasing this confused boy around. He texted back 'pervert' and I didn't text back.

Now, I can see that he was trying to tell

me to stop being pushy in a way that was funny but I just felt annoyed. I always felt that the unbearably pretty boy in these situations had all the power, I don't think I ever appreciated that I must have appeared quite confident and smart, as most of the time I just felt needy and sad.

Later, I ignored a text that was something to do with his photography and then a year or two later Arnab and I were doing another show in Oxford. Freddie texted saying he would be in the audience and asked if we'd be going out again after. I didn't reply. His brother had also contacted Arnab to say they'd be there. They were at the stage door when we finished. I said 'hello' and Freddie asked where the party was. I told him we were just going back to the hotel to sleep. He looked disappointed. We got in the car. I felt bad and asked Arnab if it was the right thing to do. He said, 'Yeah, after last time? Of course.'

One or two years later, I was sat in my flat with Arnab and some other friends, when he suddenly said out of nowhere, 'Oh, did you hear about Freddie? He killed himself.'

It felt worse than being dumped by the first person I'd loved. He wanted a friend. I kept seeing his face through the back window of the car as we drove away from the stage door. I had ignored his messages. I didn't help. I thought if I'd just kissed him without announcing I was going to try to kiss him, I could have saved him. He needed me to be assertive; I was supposed to tell him he was OK.

But what ego insanity is this? I knew there were hundreds of people who actually knew him who couldn't have done anything but I thought, The point of me, if I'm here for anything, is to help young gay people know that they're OK. To save the eighteen-year-old who wasn't saved. Why did I reject him? I tried to stop thinking about it because it was too painful. I'd failed in the only thing that meant anything to me. I was numb.

I tried not to think about the possibility that he may have been sat in the audience for that first tour where I said . . .

Is there anything worse than being
alive? Is there?

And you may think, Death . . .
death is surely going to be worse.
But death is not going to be worse
than life; death is going to be a
lot less bother.

Have you got the dentist
today? No, I'm dead, it's ideal! My
message is, if you're ever feeling
like you just can't go on, don't!
Why would you?

no self

ayahuasca

What I'm about to tell you will not sound rational, it is not rational. I tried to find peace in the rational world, I could not find it.

About six months ago now, I came back from Peru, where I drank this medicine with a shaman. This may sound like a bit of a crazy drug trip, but I promise you, it is not that.

numb

I'd been in psychotherapy for two years and while I'd begun to understand a lot of what was wrong with me, we hadn't got to the bottom of why I often felt sad for no reason. More than that, the end of my last relationship and Freddie's suicide meant I was now unable to feel anything. And I'd just met someone I liked. I wanted to feel it.

I heard about Ayahuasca at a dinner with some old school friends. I didn't really understand what Ayahuasca was but when my friend spoke about it his face beamed with such joy and enthusiasm, he looked like he was about nine years old. I asked him to send me the details and then I flew to Peru.

I find myself (now) on a spiritual journey to overcome ego, which would be great except it's such an egotistical journey to be on.

I have a friend on the same journey and it is clear yet unspoken that we are now in competition.

So I will say something like, 'I'm going to Peru next month, to visit a shaman in the rainforest. We're going to drink this plant medicine that has been used by the indigenous people for thousands of years to heal themselves.'

And he will say, 'Oh yeah, I know the guy who invented Peru.'

And he is winning but what I've realised is that any competition is ridiculous because nobody wins this thing, we all just die. So to do anything from a point of ego is absurd. To do something for just the joy of doing it, in that moment, I feel there's some integrity there. So what I thought was, If I can do everything in my life now on from a point of pure joy, then I'll be the best.

numb

I wasn't sure if what happened to me in Peru could be stand-up comedy. It was such a personal and totally peculiar thing, it had saved my life and I didn't want to diminish it. I didn't even name the plant medicine as I was concerned I would misrepresent or appropriate something that I had no right even discussing. I still don't understand what happened. It was so far from anything that makes sense in this culture, that to even begin talking about it with any authority would be ridiculous but I thought I could talk about what happened for me personally, as one particular clown with depression.

'Ayahuasca' is a thick 'brew' made from the vine *Banisteriopsis caapi* (often called caapi) and the leaf *Psychotria viridis* (known as chacruna). It tastes quite bad but you end up experiencing consciousness-expanding, life-altering 'visions' and connect to who you really are, so it feels worth it. It was unlike any consciousness-expanding substance I'd ever tried. I've enjoyed magic mushrooms in my life, because I don't do drugs, but I will if they contain magic.

On magic mushrooms, I remember saying, 'Isn't it odd how when you say to someone, "Do you wanna meet up for some dinner next Thursday?", the dinner is a lie because what you're really saying is, "It would be lovely to meet up with you." ' So why do we have to have this dinner cover? Why can't we just say, 'It would be nice to meet up with you?' And there should be a place where you can just meet, 'the meeting place', where you walk in, you sit down and just look at each other. It's truthful, it's authentic, it's beautiful. And then I thought, after about half an hour sat there, you could get a bit hungry . . . And I invented the restaurant.

do nothing

On magic mushrooms I just giggled for hours. In contrast, Ayahuasca was a traumatic, healing experience, over four ritualised ceremonies led by shamans, who had been working with the medicine for decades. We were encouraged to refer to Ayahuasca as a 'healing plant medicine', not a 'hallucinogenic drug', which has connotations of other substances that may be quite wonderful but are not used as part of a healing ritual that has been performed for thousands of years by people in the rainforest using nature alone. I did a terrifyingly minimal amount of research before I went but when I arrived I was told that this is a medicine that 'calls to you'. When my friend's story came up at dinner, it was actually the third time I'd heard the word Ayahuasca, so it made sense to me that I'd been called to the rainforest. When I told my new boyfriend this, he said, 'I keep hearing the word skiing.'

To get to the rainforest, I flew to Iquitos International Airport, as did eleven other people from around the world.

. . . All there for various different reasons, depression . . . mainly depression.

numb

The shaman, who was an American man called Don Howard, picked everyone up and escorted us to his van. He drove us to a small boat and then we sailed through the rainforest, which I found healing in itself. It reminded me of being in Thailand on my own. I wondered why I hadn't done more of this.

It became clear that I was there because I could not be in a group of people without fear. And I know that's weird, me saying that, because I do this, but this was the only way I could cope with talking to people – raised and lit.

numb

We each had our own basic hut – a single bed, a toilet and a sink. There were a few showers, along wooden walkways, which were our route to the large teepee structure where the ceremonies would take place. There was also a balcony overlooking the river where we ate and an indoor structure for the 'talking circles', which happened the day after each ceremony.

I didn't get to know anyone at first because I saw myself as separate from these other troubled loons. And in such a laid-back atmosphere, I felt incredibly tense. There was a very loose schedule and I couldn't cope. I wanted to know how long each meal or section of the retreat was going to last, so I could plan how long my 'set' was.

I took a small notebook with me.

I often have a notebook, so if anyone is looking they can think, Oh, is he lonely? Oh no, he must be a travelling genius.

numb

Unfortunately this notebook mainly reveals my desperation and need to feel it was a good idea to be alone in Peru drinking something I didn't understand. This is what I wrote. Please remember I was classically depressed.

It is clear I am here to overcome fear, anxiety, the need to control. I must let go of everything. I trust that I will be taken care of here. I just need to breathe. Accept, let go, accept, do nothing, let go, accept, do nothing, accept, let go.

I want to be here. It is important I am here. I have travelled far.

I am not an observer watching a film of characters. I am here. I am here.

I was there. I had travelled far.

I think the problem comes from the inability to just be purely in the moment without fear, I think we are all stuck in the past and looking to the future and it's in the moment where true joy exists, it's in the moment where love can occur.

I was in Paris recently with a new group of people, one of whom was a sort of kooky interesting girl, although in hindsight, not that interesting.

I always get fooled, I always think, Oh she seems fascinating. Is she, Simon? Or does she just have short hair?

Completely fascinated, I think, I'll talk to her for the rest of my life – bored after ten minutes – 'You should grow your hair and stop misleading people!'

She suggests at about three in the morning that we all run up the Champs-Élysées to the Arc de Triomphe. And I guess telling you about that now, it sounds exciting and fun, but at the time I just thought, Why would we do that? And everyone else is just at one with the moment, at one with joy, at one with the universe, and I'm there, as I'm running, thinking, Well, this will probably make a good memory. Which is living in the future, discussing the past, with someone who if they asked you 'oh what did it feel like?', you'd have to say, 'I don't know, I was thinking about what to say to you!'

do nothing

We are about to sit in a circle and tell each other about ourselves. I wonder if I can do this in an emotionally open and calm way.

I couldn't. I was funny.

I don't know what I'm afraid of. What is so terrible about silence? I panic that people won't be able to cope. That I need to take care of them. (Like my mum?) I wonder who I am, if I am not these defence mechanisms.

The first ceremony is tonight.

There were four ceremonies, in which we drank this plant medicine and in each one we were sat in a circle, in the dark. In the first one nothing much happened ... In the second one I was reborn. We don't have time to discuss what happened, but I was reborn.

numb

We now have time.

Ceremony one: we were given a small bucket to be sick in and the choice of a rocking chair or a yoga mat. I decided that I was much too cool to be sat in a rocking chair, so suffered the consequence of having to sit up straight for four hours.

Along with Don Howard, the ceremony was led by a second shaman from Peru, Don Rober. I trusted the shamans completely, even though they entered the teepee in matching outfits. We were each asked to approach them one at a time to drink. It didn't taste as bad as had been suggested. I was pleased to be there and ready for whatever was about to happen. I told myself to relax, have an open heart, do nothing, accept and let go.

Nothing happened. I couldn't let go.

I tried singing `Let It Be´ to myself.

I really wanted to throw up. Everyone else was throwing up, it was embarrassing.

I decided I must just be pure. Then remembered I came into the jungle for actual reasons and needed to purge as much as anyone, but making an effort would not work and making an effort to not make an effort would not work.

So I just started nodding my head and squeezing my ankle in time to the music. I shook back and forwards a bit and I could feel something was coming. I told myself, Let it come, let it come, because I knew I could have stopped it, which would have been more polite in normal circumstances, but buckets were provided.

So I said `come´ and it came. Not a lot of anything volume wise but it felt like something substantial had occurred. Almost instantly I felt clear, well, pure. I thought, Maybe my depression is in that bucket now. I decided to let the visions come. I tried to relax and trying to relax meant that I couldn't relax. I wondered if I'd come all this way to throw up and sit in the dark.

I could hear other people making noises that suggested they were experiencing life-changing visions and I was just sat there, singing 'Let It Be' to myself.

After a few hours, I noticed the songs that had been coming from the left of the room were now coming from the centre. Each person was having the songs sung to them whilst being hit on the head with some leaves.

I was pleased it was almost over and found being sung to and hit over the head quite nurturing. I told myself to feel that.

A candle was lit, the ceremony was over. I was ready to go but then felt horribly nauseous again. Was I about to throw up? I'd already let it go at the appropriate time and in a polite, delicate manner.

I decided I'd wait until I got back to my room. Then I remembered someone saying that if you do that, you end up with a pretty disgusting room. So I thought, Fuck it, who cares? Do it. And it came, loudly, horribly, there was a lot of it. I could hear the shaman laughing and I thought, This isn't funny, is this funny?

I didn't feel pure after the second purge, I felt ill, weak and angry at the room for doing this to me.

I walked to my room destroyed. Turned the lights on. Too bright. Turned them off. I felt dizzy. I only had the energy to brush my teeth. I crawled into bed. I noticed my right hand was shaking, like it was wondering what had just happened. I felt bad for what I'd done to my body. I said, `I'm sorry, I'm sorry, it's not your fault.'

I started having conversations with various parts of my body, until I decided I sounded like a maniac and shouldn't be separating myself from my body. I told myself to `shush, shush, shush' and eventually calmed down. I wondered who was doing this shushing. Who was shushing who?

I woke up still feeling terribly weak. On the bright side, I can't feel too anxious talking to people.

There was a flower bath to keep the medicine in the body and keep unwanted purged elements out. I thought this would be a Jacuzzi but it was a small washing-up bowl full of cold water and flowers, thrown over my near naked body, along with some more singing and leaf head-hitting.

I have no idea how I'm going to explain any of this when I get home. I'm still feeling like this will bring a new-found self that is comfortable, content, able to feel ... It's just quite a tough way of getting there.

Ceremony two:

> Second ceremony last night – part of me doesn't want to spoil it with words.

I decided to sit in a rocking chair. I wasn't going to try to *do* anything. Just listen to the music.

> I rocked in time to the music. I hadn't slept before the ceremony despite trying, so I was quite sleepy when it began, which felt good. No energy to 'do' anything.

I surrendered to the medicine and then threw up.

> I purged quite a lot and it almost felt good. I was grateful. I said, 'Thank you.'

We had been told to thank the medicine for whatever she provided. What happened next was so strange I can only apologise for not being a better writer, who could describe this experience in a way that makes sense.

> I could suddenly feel my head being moved around by what looked like large leaf hands, gently pushing and catching my head from left to right.

I was finally having 'visions'. My eyes were closed, so when I say I 'saw', it's only because I'm not sure what the correct word would be. More than seeing the visions, I was feeling them moving me, holding me.

I wasn't sure if it was just me doing the moving but it didn't feel like I was in charge any more. It felt like the rainforest knew I had bad posture and was going to fix me.

I said, 'Thank you . . . Wonderful.'

Once the big leaf hands had finished with me, I found myself in a plasma-like bubble. I didn't know where I was but it felt lovely. It was a living organism; I could see small tentacles moving with some kind of job to do, like they were making me.

I was in the womb.

It's always the womb.

I felt very safe, happy, even when I felt nauseous and needed to put my head between my legs. When I moved, the vision moved with me. I was protected in my bubble.

Then I was a baby in a pram, being rocked by my mother/mother Ayahuasca. I felt incredibly content. I was being looked after, I was safe, I was loved.

But then I heard the girl sat opposite me screaming and crying like she was being chased . . . I noticed my mother wasn't in the room any more, the rocking had stopped. I had a vision of my mother screaming and crying and another of my dad slapping her across the face. I felt myself tense over, my little shoulders rounded, my baby stomach tightened. I needed to do something to stop this man from hurting my mum.

And then something in the rainforest said to me, `You couldn't do anything. You were just a baby. You couldn't even crawl.' I sobbed and kept repeating or hearing `you were just a baby, you couldn't even crawl'. I cried and forgave my baby self for not doing anything, I cried for all the anxiety and depression that had followed. Everything pointed back to this moment. The round shoulders, the stomach problems, the shyness, the terror of going anywhere without my mum.

I thanked Ayahuasca, I said, `I know this is what I'm supposed to say but, thank you, I really do appreciate this. Thank you. Really.'*

* It is important to say that I don't recall what I've described here actually happening in real life. What matters, I think, is the perception this baby had of something scary, which he felt was his responsibility to stop.

I said I would like to be able to sit up straight. The reply was `then sit up!´ and beyond my control, my hands came together in my hair and pulled my head up, as if I was about to be scalped. I was sat upright. I danced in the chair and cried. The depression had been unlocked. I was free. I had found the root of the shyness, of the reason I ever needed to be funny. It was the key to my entire ridiculous personality. I´m OK with my personality but sometimes it´s nice to have it as a choice rather than a panic button. To choose to be quiet or funny in a situation is more fun than having to make people laugh so they don´t hurt you.

And then, although no one had said that this was a place where I could contact the dead, I said I would like to see Freddie.

Freddie appeared, relaxed, smiling, cute. Better than the sad, anxious boy I met in Oxford. He looked like he was OK. I can´t remember what we said at first but quite soon I asked him sadly, `Am I just talking to myself here?´ And he said `just go with it´, which made me laugh, and I carried on. I started asking him questions about why he had killed himself and then I realised I was rambling on and on, in the same way that I´d rambled on in the hotel room, when I should have just had the confidence to be with him and kiss him. And then he kissed me. The room spun around us and, still in the kiss, I heard his voice say, 'I would have killed myself anyway.'

I cried a lot.

I asked, 'Why . . .? Why did you . . .?'

He shrugged and said, 'This is your time.'

'But, so are you . . . are you gay or . . .?'
He said, 'Where I am now, it's not really a thing.'

It was so good to see him again.

Everything seemed to finish about half an hour before the candle was lit. I said, 'Thank you, it's so much, it's too much.' And then, 'Is there anything else? Because I'm here.' She stroked my body gently and said, 'Rest now. Rest now.'

I'd always said, whatever happened in the past, it was perfect ... And something in the rainforest, after I'd drank this medicine, said to me, 'It wasn't perfect, though, was it?'

And it was such a relief, to accept that. I said, 'No . . . what was it, then?'

And it said, 'It was what it was.'

And I said, 'But it's been very useful, for what I do in my career.'

And it said, 'What you do is what you do, it is not a big deal', which was a great relief but also very insulting.

numb

At the second 'talking circle' I could feel myself emerging as the person I'd hoped I might become, beyond my 'temporary personality before I get to the good one'.

In the first one I'd avoided eye contact with anyone and only felt OK when people laughed. This time I made a point of grounding myself. I told everyone what I'd seen and I cried.

To cry in front of people was incredible, to see that no one would feel uncomfortable, that I didn't have to take care of anyone.

Ceremony three:

The first ceremony taught me surrender. I was reborn in the second and in the fourth I became a man.

Nothing happened in the third.

Ceremony four:

As we drank for the final time, I could feel myself being quite solitary and missing out on being a member of this tribe. My healing had been deeply personal but I was ready now to be with these people. I told myself, 'Be in the room.'

Even before drinking the medicine, I started singing in my head, the prayer that a bar mitzvah boy sings before he reads his portion or the Torah – 'Ba-r'chu et a-do-nai ha-m'vo-rach.

Ba-ruch a-do-nai ha-m'vo-rach l'o-lahm va-ed'.
And then I became a cat.

To my left in the circle was an attractive American who I felt had also become a cat, I heard him purring. And I started thinking about him in the ceremony but felt ashamed of these sexual thoughts I was having. And then something in the medicine said to me, 'Why do you feel ashamed? You are a strong sexy cat.'

And so I turned to him, beyond my own control, and rather than *saying* something like 'maybe we should kiss', I just did this motion . . . [beckons him]

And then he, not his physical head, but his spirit cat energy, landed in my palm and we kissed and I giggled because I felt embarrassed and then the medicine said, 'Why do you feel embarrassed? Look, he enjoyed it.'

I looked over: he did enjoy it. But he also looked quite shocked, so I said, 'DO NOT BE CONCERNED! This was just a moment between us; it is not your path. CONTINUE!'

numb

That was just one of many lessons in how to be in a group without anxiety.

All my fears came up in various forms. Each time I was terrified and then realised that by accepting them they would disappear. At one point my fist tried to plunge its way into my mouth. I was scared I was going to break my jaw and then somehow understood that the fear was only in my head (much more than my fist). I surrendered and let my arm do what it wanted. It pulled away.

I found myself in a vast dome of breasts. And as one of the many breasts moved towards my face, my thumb made its way into my mouth, acting as a physical surrogate for the nipple. I started sucking my thumb, gulping down all the wisdom that Mother Nature wanted to feed me. I didn't want it to end. The thumb started coming out of my mouth, as the huge breast pulled away. So I bit down on my thumb but then heard a firm voice say, 'It's enough now.' I apologised to Mother Nature for biting her nipple. I felt I had been taught the lesson of 'enough'. I thought, Maybe as a baby I bit my mother's nipples so I apologised to her too.

I was feeling tired and then decided, Why feel tired? You are here. Use this time. I said to the rainforest, 'Tell me everything now, for I will not return!'

At one point everyone in the room became a circle of gods, sat on thrones, and then Richard Dawkins walked in. He looked terribly shocked by what he was seeing. I laughed but then felt bad. As one of the gods, I said to him, 'You have done great work, Richard, you were one of my best.' Which seems arrogant and absurd now but at the time, it felt like an incredibly kind thing to say.

When the last ceremony ended I could still feel the medicine inside me. I felt these urges that I had to follow – they said, 'We need to feel the rain on your body.' I stood completely naked in the rain and felt comfortable in my body for the first time of my life. I then heard, 'We need you to dance.' I said, 'OK, but I think I need to do a poo first. Should I do the poo and then dance? Or dance now?' The rainforest replied, '*You* don't *do* the poo!'

It suddenly hit me like a revelation: I don't do the poo. The most I do is *allow* the poo. I thought, This is so important – I can't wait to tell the people.

Because it hadn't occurred to me
that the body is just breathing itself –
we're only getting in the way . . . We
should just be eating when we are
hungry, no other reason, sleeping when
we are tired, and having sex when there
is the urge – and consent – but that
is it.

to be free

I went to get my headphones and I put on some
Michael Jackson. As the music started to play, for
the first time I noticed these wet curls in front of
my eyes, of course mine from the rain, but in that
moment I thought – I *am* Michael Jackson.

numb

After the last Ayahuasca ceremony, I felt so
grateful for what these leaves had allowed in me.
I felt a great urge to hug a tree but couldn't find
one, so hugged a wooden post.

Even beyond any duty to repay nature, it suddenly seemed so obvious that we can't continue to live as if we are separate from a planet that we are sitting on. Ayahuasca looked after me. She made me better. I don't feel separate any more, I feel held.

I learned to *feel* in the rainforest, to just *be* rather than think, to just exist in the moment, instinctively. I asked Ayahuasca, 'What are we here for? What is the point of this? Is it just joy, everything else seems ridiculous, is it just joy, is it just joy? Is it joy?!' And then a tired-looking Gorilla appeared before me, and said, 'Yes it's all joy.'

And I wrote down 'joy confirmed'.

numb

When I got back to my room, I tried to sleep but the wisdom kept coming and I wrote as much of it down as I could. I didn't mention any of these things in my stand-up show. I thought they were holy sentences that shouldn't be mocked. Each sentence was written on its own page, in capital letters and circled.

> INSTINCTS ARE RIGHT.
> WE ARE EARTH.
> MUST HELP GORILLAS.

I had a second vision of a gorilla who said, 'You need to help us', which I think meant, help nature, animals, the planet. I couldn't figure out how to help the gorillas so I set up a direct debit to Fauna & Flora International.

> WEAR YOUR GLASSES – SYMBOL OF
> WISDOM.
> LEARN FROM YOUNG PEOPLE.
> THEY ARE THE NEW BATCH.
> READ THE TORAH – YOU WROTE IT.

My head was buzzing, I was lying on the bed, wide awake and then for around three seconds there was a burst of heavy rain. It felt like nature was saying, 'Shussssssssssh.' Like the rain was stroking my head and suggesting it was time to sleep. As soon as I calmed down, the rain stopped. I wondered if I could make the rain come again but didn't want to test it.

Before I could fall asleep, I felt quite curious to see what would happen if I looked in a mirror. I swayed forwards and backwards, looking deeply into my own eyes and then, in a flash, my face froze, like a mask and I heard the words, YOU ARE GOD LOOKING THROUGH YOU.

In the moment, it made complete sense and resolved everything – the self is a construct, the body a vessel for some kind of consciousness to experience itself for some reason, or no reason. My face, my personality, my name, anything to do with me is not who I am. The reality of 'me' is something within or underneath or beyond all of that silliness.

And when I am anxious, depressed or lonely, it is a transient bit of nonsense, covering the truth of what I actually am – the beyond-words thing that is actually me. I don't know what this thing beyond the 'I' is, but the fact that 'I' am the one asking the question is probably the reason. In the past, when I've heard people say (or even when I've said) that 'everything is connected', I couldn't really *feel* what that meant but now, in my body, I get that I'm a small part of something much deeper and more expansive than anything my ego could come up with. Looking back through the stories in this book, when I've suffered it has often been the result of my mind creating a desire to get somewhere other than the moment I'm in. When I'm able to surrender to what *is*, I feel an ease and flow that doesn't seem to happen when I'm driven by my own lunacy. I'm aware that my ego probably likes the idea of having this brilliant connection to everything but I don't know what we can do about that.

When I arrived home, something had clearly changed in me. I was wandering along a country path with some friends, a dog came out of nowhere and started barking at us, it was all quite scary and my friend said, 'Let's just keep walking.' I would have kept walking in the past; I would have made a little joke so we could all cope a bit better. I stood there and stared at the dog. Until he walked away. And what a stupid dog, because I'm a cat.

numb

I wasn't broken any more. Ayahuasca got to the core of how my identity was constructed. I found a strength I didn't know I had. When I feel sad now, I know it's not because I'm a broken human being, it's because it is one of the emotions that human beings feel.

after ayahuasca

A wound that needed status to avoid intimacy has been healed. I was healthy, I was in a relationship with someone who had a happy childhood, how would I now find the motivation to earn attention from strangers? I didn't seem to have depression any more, yet I still had a mortgage. I was becoming a normal person.

I was happy. I felt alive and had no idea what to do. There wasn't a clear spiritual path to follow when I arrived home and my insecure little ego monster made a powerful comeback. Feeling betrayed by the joy-filled maniac I'd become, it grabbed me by the throat and said, 'You need to break America, become a highly respected dramatic actor and write and direct a feature film, otherwise people will stop loving you.'

Deep down I knew I'd found something that transcended all of that silliness but I couldn't just keep looking at my face in the mirror, remembering that I was 'God looking through me', so I went to America.

THE CAREER

It should just be about the joy at this
point, right? But you know, once you
attain some status, you then have to retain
that status. I decided two or three years
ago that it would be very important for me
to go to America and become accepted as a
comedian there. Only because *other* people
had done that – I thought it would start to
get a bit embarrassing for me if I didn't.
Who am I if I don't do that – some *regional*
comedian who's a bit famous on one tiny
island? And if I go anywhere else, I'm –
I'm *you*!

   I did this residency in New York
City, and it should have been pure joy to be
doing this show for three months and
everything became about my ego's need to
get somewhere. And finally somebody said to
me, 'Simon, you're doing a show in New
York – if you're not happy now, you'll never
be happy.' And I thought: I'll never be happy!

to be free

Ayahuasca had provided a powerful burst of enlightenment but without some kind of daily practice I occasionally fell back into existential misery. Because it doesn't matter what you do, what you achieve, the ending is always the same. You win the Olympics – you die; you buy your dream home – you die; you're pregnant – you both die.

And forget that we're all going to die; we're going to live for so long. Someone said to me, 'In forty years you'll be seventy-seven,' and I thought, How long is this going to go on for?

It used to be, you were born, married at twelve, by sixteen you were dead and now you have to keep doing new and endlessly impressive things because of the horror of being asked at parties, 'What are you up to at the moment?'

'Isn't it enough that I grew up in Essex and now I'm at this party in Hampstead? I did it.'

It's difficult to stay connected to your joyful, true self if you watch the news, so I've stopped doing that. Because it isn't even the news. What they give us is the worst most awful things that have happened in the world that day. That's not an accurate representation of what's going on on our planet. If it was, I could watch it because it would be, 'Hi, how are you? Did you have a nice day? The news team – we had a barbecue . . . So what have we got for you? The sun came up, again, grass continued to grow, now some people have died, but you never met. So you can't feel bad about that and don't feel bad about not feeling bad, that would be silly . . . And also everything's being dealt with by experts.

'If you're still watching, we can now go live to our Middle East correspondent, Harold. Harold, what can you tell us?'

'Well, it's just ridiculous.'

'Thank you, Harold.'

numb

Pursuing recognition as a stand-up in America worked out quite well, in that I was performing sold-out shows and appearing on late-night chat shows. But being a stand-up comedian was only going to get me so far and it suddenly became very important to become the new Cate Blanchett.

I started reading scripts that meant nothing to me, being very charming in meetings that exhausted me and demoted stand-up to a stepping stone, rather than the place where I felt most free.

> And I should be over all this ego now, I really thought I was over vanity, and then I went to see a low-budget film that I was in and it was the first time I'd seen my face on the cinema screen. A lot of actors can't even look at themselves, they won't watch the films. I came out of there thinking, My face should always be that big.
>
> *to be free*

I got a hint that I didn't actually want to be a transformative actor after reading an interview that Eddie Redmayne gave about his year-long preparation for playing Stephen Hawking. I was aware that most actors would be thinking, I'd love to have the opportunity to do something so challenging. And I thought, Who the hell can be bothered with this?

I felt a bit better recently – I'd just finished writing a film and I thought, OK, we're OK – what's better than a film? And then my friend Russell Brand decided to start a revolution. I didn't know that was an option.

We were both trained clowns, and then he goes, 'Yeah, I enjoy this clown work but I think I'm probably also Gandhi. What are you up to, Simon?'

'Oh, I've just finished writing a film.'

'Oh, that's good. I'm trying to save the world from economic and ecological disaster. What's the film about?'

'Me?'

I had an idea for a TV show recently and it was such a relief, to have come up with something new. And then after about half an hour of thinking about this great new idea, I realised it was *Brass Eye*. I didn't have an idea, I had a memory.

And it's not like you even get what you used to get in show business, which

was a feeling of real elevation. Now I get
messages on Twitter that say: 'Can you let
us know what time the show finishes, we
have to book a babysitter.' I'm the star!
Why do they think that's OK? You can't
just talk to me!

to be free

Near the end of the most recent tour of America,
I met someone with incredible posture and eyes
full of actual joy. I went up to him and said,
'How are you doing this?'

He told me about his spiritual journey and
I thought if I paid enough attention, he would
provide the path that I required, post Ayahuasca.
I told him I'd begun to enjoy meditating, that it was
no longer something I felt obliged to do. He said,
'Do you know what that is? You've gone from
discipline, to blissipline.'

I laughed and he didn't know why. He
just looked at me with his silly, joy-filled eyes,
thinking, Why are you laughing? Don't you think
you've gone to blissipline?

He was just another lovely and ridiculous

human being. I must stop looking for a leader, nobody is outside of ridiculous.

Eventually I was so drained from trying to be loved internationally, I had a minor breakdown in a hotel room in LA. The meeting I had with an actor who I thought would be perfect to play the vulnerable young love interest in the film I'd written had been cancelled at the last minute and I was suddenly in the terrifying position of being alone with nothing to do.

I watched some Michael Jackson videos on YouTube. I found an advert he did for Pepsi in 1991 that I'd never seen before. It's just Michael, sat on his own, playing a grand piano in what feels like a very peaceful room. He's singing 'I'll Be There' and looks content. 'I reach out my hand to you, I have faith in all you do . . .' And just as he's about to sing 'Just call my name . . .', the film cuts to a wide shot of the room and behind Michael is the young 'Jackson Five' Michael, singing to his adult self, 'Just call my name and I'll be there'. I started crying and I wasn't sure why. I laid myself down on the bed in the foetal position. Something about this boy singing to his adult self that if he needed him he would be there, and adult

Michael, now in this peaceful room, able to sing back to his younger self that he would be there for him too. I realised this was the connection I had lost. I was so embarrassed by my younger self and I blamed his ambition for my dissatisfaction.

Somehow in this moment I realised that while my personality was a construction of various defence mechanisms, abandoning them at this point was rather ungrateful. I do like being funny, I could carry on being funny. Still crying half an hour later, I said out loud to my abandoned, child self, 'I'm sorry, thank you, I'm so sorry.' I felt him say that it was OK and then he told me I should probably write all this down, just in case. I started laughing. It felt so good to be laughing with him.

I later realised that fame was not what I wanted, it was connection. There's a sweet spot for fame. I really just want to be anonymous enough that I can go to a restaurant and eat with the person that I am with, but not so anonymous that *someone* in that restaurant doesn't tell me that something I've done is brilliant.

THE BOYFRIEND

My boyfriend and I have been together for almost six years. We met a few months before I went to Peru and along with having to work out how to be in show business without a wound, I had to discover how to be in a healthy relationship. He's very different to anyone I've been with before, in that he's not someone I think I need to save.

It isn't easy writing about this relationship because I'm in it right now and it seems to be working. I don't feel the need to deconstruct it, I want to protect it. We talk about everything, so I don't spend as much time worrying about who I am in my head. This makes me happy but possibly makes the rest of the chapter slightly less funny. There is also another person to consider when deciding how honest I can be about us but thankfully he's also quite into the truth.

I think it works because, amongst other things, we talk about other people we find attractive. I don't know if that's particularly revolutionary, but I was in a relationship years ago where there was such insecurity, I ended up having to say, 'I don't think anyone's attractive . . . and it's weird because before I met you . . . but, they must have all moved.'

We'll go to see a dance performance and talk about the flexibility of the dancers and the magic of the movements. And we're both comfortable knowing that what we're saying is, we'd like to take one home and ruin his life.

And we should be able to do that because the tickets are so expensive.

We were in France recently, and it really is the most authentic, beautiful relationship I've ever been in. And there were croissants . . . And yet, I fall asleep next to him in France and I have a dream that I'm in a dungeon being seduced by a wet slut boy.

And not wet from water, covered in lubricant. And I should have known it was a dream, because it was too much lubricant! And I said to him, 'Listen, I'm in a relationship. I can't really get involved with you here.' But I couldn't stop him, because he was such a slippery slut.

And I had such a great time, but then afterwards I thought, Oh no, what have I done? I've betrayed the best relationship I've ever been in, what am I going to do? And then I woke up, everything was fine. But for the next week, all I could think was, I really love that sex dungeon. Is that who I really am? Because you can't argue with the unconscious, and everything now in life just seems so appropriate and polite: 'Do you want another croissant, Simon?' 'No! I want to shove this pain au chocolat up your bottom! Your body's so dry!'

But as much as I loved that sex dungeon, I knew that it wasn't ideal long-term. Still I can't stop thinking about it – it feels like that's the truth of me, I'm this animal who wants to be there and everything else is just some societal expectation. And then I go to my boyfriend's mother's birthday dinner, and his little brother gives this beautiful speech

about how much he loves his parents . . .
He talks about how much he appreciates
them for accepting their children no
matter who they turned out to be. And I
start crying, I guess thinking about the
acceptance here, in contrast to the
problems I've had over the years with my
own family. And I turn to my boyfriend and
I say, 'This is better than the sex dungeon.'

to be free

My boyfriend's family were completely accepting
of me. I found this strange and unnerving. It's a
bit like what happened with my little brother's
pet hamster. He never cleaned the cage and so
the hamster grew accustomed to the dirt. Then
one day my brother cleaned the cage and the
hamster died of shock.

It took me a long time to realise I could
tell my boyfriend anything. A few years in, I got
into a bit of a pickle at the Edinburgh Fringe
Festival. Walking out of my show, I was
approached by a group of girls and one boy. The

boy was quite nervous and beautiful. I had a sense his friends were trying to push him towards me. I chatted to them for a while and thought about what could happen before walking away. Doing the right thing that night began to eat away at me.

It took me three days before I could finally say to my boyfriend, 'I need to talk to you about something that didn't happen in Edinburgh.' I felt terrible for even bringing it up. I thought about how awful it would have been if my grandpa had ever said to my grandma that one of his taxi passengers had come on to him and that having spent so many years doing 'The Knowledge', it was a shame not to take the opportunity.

I told him I couldn't stop thinking about it. He looked very serious, for quite a long time and then said, 'I'm very pleased that you've told me how you're feeling. I guess what you're saying is, you're a human being.'

'What do you mean?'

He said, 'I suppose I also see people I find attractive.'

I said, 'Right, but I couldn't have slept with him?'

He said, 'No.'

Then added, 'But it does feel like a shame.'

We hugged and decided we'd both have a good think about what we wanted and after a few days of discussion, came to the conclusion that we didn't want an open relationship because it sounded a little tiring but if someone insanely beautiful just presented themselves to you, it would be a shame not to say 'yes'. So we *don't* sleep with people outside of the relationship but, in principle, we *could* if it was unmissable and didn't require any effort. And if such a thing happened, we could talk about it and see how we felt.

And then this happened. About a year and a half ago we went to a party together, where we discovered something called MDMA. Oh my God. What kind of a country is this where you can legally buy cigarettes, alcohol and sugar but it's illegal to be *happy*?

This was the last ever party at the house where the cool parties had happened all those years ago. It was so lovely to be there with someone and without anxiety. We were sat with a couple of other boys – Harry, an artist we both fancy, and Stephen, the boy I should have kissed years ago but didn't because I thought he was asthmatic. I felt this pure bliss and couldn't stop smiling. It was like being a baby; I just wanted to touch people. I was staring into Harry's eyes and pulling on his earlobe for maybe an hour.

After a while he said to me, 'Do you want me to kiss you?'

I said, 'Yes! But you must also kiss my boyfriend.' He agreed so I said, 'Quick! Harry will kiss you now!'

I watched these two beautiful men kissing and then my boyfriend and I looked at each other and thought, This is a good party.

Then another friend squatted down in front of us, the only person who had taken cocaine. She was outraged by the kissing and I said, 'You're at the wrong party, cokey!' She took Harry away which was sad but I felt like all the boundaries of society had disappeared, all the boundaries of my personality had dissolved, there were no boundaries. Then I said out loud, 'I'm going to hold Stephen's hand.' And Stephen pulled his hand away. I thought, Oh, there are boundaries. I didn't feel rejected though, it was just a thing that hadn't happened. I thought, I'll just hold my own hand, which felt wonderful.

Then the next day, I did the most brilliant poos. They were just slowly gliding out of me, like elegant canoes. And so many, like they'd been waiting, through fifteen years of anxiety and something said, 'We can leave now!'

And two days after that, I couldn't stop crying.

It took me a few more days to realise that I should feel quite angry that this medicine isn't available in pharmacies. MDMA has been used in couples' counselling; it's the pure form of ecstasy, the original name for which was 'empathy'. In this country it is illegal to have empathy. I've tried many forms of healing but it was the illegal ones that really did the job. Psychotherapy was incredible but it was Ayahuasca that actually got to the root of my depression. Magic mushrooms made me realise how ridiculous everything is and I became funnier, which has been very good for society. And I love having acupuncture but it hasn't ever helped me and my boyfriend kiss Harry.

For a while I thought the only problem in my life, was not being on MDMA.

I read *To Kill a Mockingbird* at school. There was a character who went on this heroic journey of purification, she knew she was dying and wanted to give up her addiction of morphine before the moment came. I remember thinking, What a stupid thing to do! If I knew I had a month to live, one of the things I would *take up* would be morphine. I had it for an operation – it's like a hug from the inside. It feels like love, but with none of the bother. You wouldn't give it up, you'd say, 'Double the morphine and bring me Atticus Finch!'

numb

But in the end I realised you only really need to take MDMA once because it's such a great teacher. (I've taken it more than once.) It allowed an intimacy that I didn't know was possible. I was so shy as a child, so ashamed as an adult, and this medicine dissolved everything. I could just *be* with another person, touch another person, without pretending to be someone better. And with that awareness, at least I can now arrive somewhere between the effects of MDMA and my regular personality.

I suppose this hunger for connection is what this has all been about. To be shy or depressed is to be disconnected, to be able to express your entire, ridiculous self is to be free.

We need to feel connected to who we really are, which is each other, nature, the universe, or at least be in a relationship with another person. Otherwise we feel alone and we eat everything.

I was in a hotel room recently, completely alone, and there was a chance my boyfriend could meet me on this holiday, for the weekend, and he couldn't.

So, the first thing I do when I get to this hotel room is I open the minibar out of curiosity. But there's nothing in that minibar for me. I don't drink and I'm a vegan so it wasn't an act of curiosity it was an act of pure loneliness. I then start opening every drawer in the room, hoping to find a little friend, somewhere?

I order a salad from room service. The reason I became vegan, by the way, is because last year I became addicted to chocolate cake and I needed a label to stop that from happening. Sometimes you need a label – the only way to not drink at a party is to be a recovering alcoholic. Because people say, 'Do you want a drink?' And if you say, 'I'm a recovering alcoholic,' they say, 'Oh, fair enough, sorry.' Otherwise it's, 'Do you want a drink?' 'No thank you.' 'Have a drink!' I feel like these people, their only aim is to make everyone into an alcoholic, and when they meet one they think, Oh, you're done, fine.

I think the reason they started giving us popcorn in cinemas is so all our senses are stimulated. Not just sight and sound but taste, touch, smell. All senses taken care of and then you can't really think. So you're sort of happy. We've been encouraged over time to numb our feelings . . . Buy this alcohol, you won't need to feel anxious; buy this ice cream, you don't have to feel sad . . . But we must feel and maybe there could be an advert that says, 'Hey, maybe you need a good cry. You're doing really well . . . The source of you is pure love.' I don't know who would pay for that advert.

I finish my salad, the film continues, but that isn't enough for me. Just the sight and sound. So I see the bread that they've brought up with the salad. Which I didn't order. I don't eat bread, because at some point I might want to be a good father.

But because I'm alone and it's there I'm now spreading butter on the bread. I'm eating all the bread and now I can't stop thinking about the chocolate in the minibar. I can't stop thinking about it. The only way to stop thinking about it is to get it out of the room, just get it out of the room and the only way I could do that is to put it in my mouth.

I ate all the chocolate in the minibar and that's why he needed to be there with me on that holiday. And I'm texting things like, 'It would be so lovely if you could come for the weekend, it would be really delightful.' That's not what I mean. What I mean is, 'Marry me, it's an emergency!'

We need to *feel* as human beings or we will consume and consume until there's nothing left. Why did we almost destroy the earth? Because we felt alone and it was there. But we are not alone; we're so profoundly connected to each other, to nature.

Last week I ate an apple. Do you know what I mean?

numb

I'm finding it hard to accept this book is finished. I wonder what I've left out, if I've gone as deep as I could have with a little more time or distance. The main question that kept coming up as I was writing was: 'What is this?' I couldn't stop thinking about how real my past thoughts and feelings seemed to be at the time and how silly they appear now. It made me question how much of my present experience would, with enough time, seem completely absurd. I imagine all of it.

What are any of us doing?

When my grandma died I remember looking at an old photograph my grandpa had taken of her. She's sitting on a rock on a beach, smiling into the camera. I stared at the photograph for a long time, looking for something meaningful, for an explanation of human existence. She was here and now she's not here. That was all I could come up with. She was here and now she's not here.

Maybe the only thing to do while we're alive on this planet with no clear idea why, is to hold each other until we feel a bit less troubled. The final story in this book is about being naked in a room with some other naked people. Thank you for reading.

My boyfriend and I recently went on a road trip across the west coast of America. A friend of ours had told us about a sex party happening in one of the states we were visiting. A real-life orgy in someone's apartment. If the sex dungeon dream was about anything, it was about craving stability, love and intimacy, but also, occasionally, in the middle of all the comfort and the joy, screaming out, 'Shouldn't we be at an orgy, more often than never?'

So we decided to go to an orgy.

However, a week earlier, another friend invited us to a one-off club night happening in Silver Lake, LA, where, incredibly, one of the rooms turned into a sex party. Suddenly what began as people dancing became people taking off their clothes and touching each other. It was quite overwhelming and we weren't sure how involved we should get. We thought we'd stick together and perhaps, if we just took our tops off and kissed each other in the middle of all this activity, people would gather around us and applaud. We did some cautious touching of other bodies. I touched a bottom so hard it was like a cupboard. Yet oddly, as someone who often thinks, We're all animals, why aren't we all just naked and having sex all the time?, once everyone was just naked and having sex, I really wished someone was wearing a hat.

I learned that I really like 'story' and the intimacy that comes from telling each other who we are. My favourite part of the evening was talking to someone who still had his clothes on and looked as nervous as us. At the end of the night, having spent many years saying, 'Why aren't we at an orgy? We should be at an orgy, why isn't this an orgy?', I ended up thinking, Oh God, next week we've got another orgy.

ACKNOWLEDGEMENTS

Special thanks to:
Susannah Otter
Daniel Chandler
Will Attenborough
Tracey MacLeod
Rowan Yapp
Sophie Crawford
Meredith Churchill
Matthew Beard